'Til Death Do Us Part?
Written by Kathy Donatini

This book is dedicated to:

my husband, Steve, whose life ended unexpectedly on March 14, 1998. The loss of a spouse is a very unique experience. When you lose a child or a parent or even when you are dying yourself, you turn to your spouse for comfort and support. There is nothing else that can compare to this type of understanding. After years of being together, no words are necessary. You know each other so well that you just instinctively meet each other's needs. Sometimes it is to be left alone, sometimes it is to be held, sometimes it is to cry and grieve and sometimes it is to remember and laugh. What do you do when the person who always comforted you is the reason for your pain? So many times, I longed to feel your arms around me just one more time. Little did I know that you were right there beside me all along. Thank you for guiding me through my awakening.

ℒ𝑜𝑠𝑠

I was startled from my sleep by the sound of the phone ringing. Confused, I sat straight up in bed and glanced over at the clock above me on the headboard. The numbers 3:32 seemed to be a much brighter red than usual.

The phone next to our bed hadn't been working quite right so I walked down the short flight of stairs that led to the kitchen to answer it. I had gotten out of bed too quickly and had to sit down on the bottom stair to take the call.

The words I heard are forever etched in my memory. **"Mrs. Donatini, this is the hospital calling. I'm afraid your husband, Steve, has taken a turn for the worse and we feel you should get here as soon as possible."**

The events of the next hour were a blur to me. I called my daughter, Kym, and asked her to come over to the house to stay with Sean and Brittany while I went to the hospital. She only lived 10 minutes away, but the wait seemed like hours.

Unsure of what was awaiting me at the hospital, I called my sister, Margie, and asked her if she would meet me there. Just as I hung up the phone, Kym arrived with her husband, Joe. He said he would stay with the kids so that Kym could go with me and we rushed out the door.

I sped toward the hospital on deserted streets. I don't even remember the route I took or whether or not Kym and I spoke to each other. Thoughts raced through my mind as I desperately tried to make sense out of what was happening.

I heard someone coming up the back stairs that led up to my office. All the employees used this entrance because we parked our cars just outside the door. Somehow I knew it would be my husband, Steve's, face that would appear from around the corner. His ascent was slow, his breathing was heavy and I could hear the familiar sound of the cough he had been fighting for the past six months.

I looked back over my shoulder and saw him leaning against the wall trying to catch his breath. His overcoat was hanging over his arm and his tie was loose around his neck. He was pale and clammy and obviously exhausted from the short climb. His raspy voice was barely audible when he asked if I could get away for lunch.

He'd had an appointment with his physician, whom I shall call Dr. Keller, earlier that morning and, as usual, they had been running behind schedule. Despite several different rounds of various types of antibiotics and antihistamines and a steroid called Prednisone, his condition seemed to be getting worse by the day. At his last appointment, Steve told Dr. Keller that he had been experiencing some reflux and stomach pain and that the slightest bit of food left him feeling as though he were full. My father had suffered from a hiatal hernia and had experienced similar symptoms so I had told

Steve to ask Dr. Keller to run the necessary tests to check it out. Dr. Keller indicated that it was doubtful that Steve was suffering from a hiatal hernia, but said he would send him for x-rays anyway.

We sat across from each other at lunch discussing his appointment. Steve explained to me that they had, in fact, found a hiatal hernia at the base of his esophagus. Dr. Keller suggested he tilt the head of our bed up a little to help keep the stomach acid from traveling up his esophagus. He gave him free samples of an antacid and told him to schedule a follow-up appointment for three months.

I had been Steve's wife for over 20 years and he knew what my reaction would be. My voice grew louder and I asked, "That was it? Come back in three months. What about your cough? Did he notice that you could barely breath? He can't just keep treating the symptoms." His tired eyes reached out to mine in the hope of finding some compassion. Dr. Keller had been his physician for many years and Steve had always trusted his judgment. However, looking into his weary face, I could see that the pain had become unbearable. He agreed that maybe Dr. Keller didn't know what he was doing. He said he didn't care who he had to see or what he had to do. He would go along with whatever I suggested. He just wanted to feel better.

I would find out much later, from a notation in Steve's medical file, that Dr. Keller had questioned whether Steve could have possibly developed an allergic reaction to his blood pressure medicine and considered looking into doing an allergy workup at some time down the road should the problems persist. Maybe we were right, maybe he truly had no clue what was wrong with Steve.

Steve called Dr. Keller when he got back to work and asked to be referred to a specialist. A cat scan of his lung was arranged for Friday and an appointment was made for him to see a pulmonary specialist on the following Monday.

3

Steve went to the appointment on Monday alone and, when he came home that night, he said that the pulmonary specialist had told him that the cat scan did show something, but he wasn't sure what. The specialist said there was a possibility of tuberculosis and he asked Steve if he had ever worked around birds. His x-rays indicated the possibility of a virus which was caused by bird droppings. He asked Steve to have an outpatient bronchoscopy done the next day so he could get a better look.

I took Steve to the hospital on my way to work the next morning and stayed with him until he was registered and taken to a room. I kissed him goodbye thinking, "Good, maybe now, at last, someone will figure out what is really going on that is making Steve so sick. Even if it turns out to be tuberculosis, at least we will know for sure and they can start treating it."

When I picked him up later that afternoon, he was still a little groggy from the anesthesia, but he seemed to be in good spirits. I took him home and got him settled and he told me he was sleepy and suggested that I go back to work. He said I shouldn't worry about him and that he would be fine alone. He just wanted to rest.

After work, I picked up Sean and Brittany from school, fed them supper, helped them with their homework, gave them baths and put them to bed. It was around 8:30 p.m. and Steve was still asleep. He had stirred a few times, but never truly woken up.

Sometime during the wee hours of the morning, I became aware that Steve wasn't lying next to me in our bed. I quietly called out his name and found him standing next to the bed pacing back and forth holding his right side. His face was very pale and he was having extreme difficulty breathing.

I wanted to rush him right to the hospital, but he was adamant that I not wake up Sean and Brittany in the middle of the night. I sat with him for three agonizing hours until about 6:30 when he finally agreed to let me call Dr. Keller's office. The answering service took the message and told me that someone would call us right back.

The few minutes it took for Dr. Keller to call seemed to stretch on for hours. I explained the circumstances to him and asked him if he could possibly meet us at the hospital. He seemed reluctant to meet us and said that he felt that I was overreacting and suggested we just wait until the following day when the biopsy results would be back. He stated that the HMO would not approve admitting Steve to the hospital without a diagnosis. He eventually said that I should take Steve to the emergency room if I really felt it was necessary for someone to see him.

I suspected that Steve's lung had been nicked during the bronchoscopy the previous morning and wanted to know what was causing him to have such difficulty breathing. I called the pulmonary specialist who had arranged for the procedure and asked him to send over an order for an x-ray.

When we arrived at the radiology department, they immediately took the x-ray of Steve's lungs. We were told to wait in the lobby until the pulmonary specialist could come over to read the x-rays and talk to us. Steve was still having such trouble breathing that I decided to walk across the street and try to catch the specialist before he left his office.

He told us that the x-ray showed absolutely no change from the one they did following the procedure the day before. However, since he wasn't sure what was causing Steve's breathing problems, he wanted to admit Steve to the hospital for observation.

Once settled in his room, Steve convinced me to go on to work until he called with any news. He looked so tired and was really on edge so I left, hoping he would get some rest. After all, he was in the hospital now. Everything would be just fine.

I had hardly sat down at my desk when the phone rang. It was Steve saying that they were taking him back into surgery and could I please hurry right back. In all the years that I had known him, I can honestly say that this was the first time I had ever heard him sound frightened. He only spoke to me for a few seconds, but there was a sense of urgency and agitation in his voice that convinced me that something was terribly wrong.

I flew out the door without explanation. It couldn't have taken me more than 15 minutes to get back to the hospital, but, when I arrived, Steve had already been taken to surgery. The nurse said that they had decided to do a deeper biopsy and that the surgery should only take about two hours. She very kindly escorted me to the surgery waiting room and explained that I would be informed of his condition as soon as the procedure was over.

As I sat waiting in that crowded room, filled with families making small talk while they waited to hear how their loved ones were doing, questions raced through my mind. Why did they have to rush him into surgery before I could get there? Did they actually find something wrong on the x-ray and just not tell me? Why did they need to do a deeper biopsy and why right this minute? Had the first biopsy come back positive? Were they trying to correct an earlier mistake before we found out about it?

Time went by so slowly as the minutes dragged into hours. The not knowing was unbearable. I was all alone in a room full of strangers. I tried to find something interesting to read in the outdated magazines that were scattered around the room on tables covered with empty coffee cups and dusty plastic flower arrangements.

I hated not being able to get answers to my questions. I wasn't used to not being able to control things and patience had never been one of my strong points. It took everything I had not to find a nurse and demand answers.

The hours ticked by without any word from inside the operating room. It was almost 5:00 p.m. and Sean and Brittany needed to be picked up from their daycare by 5:30. I would not leave the hospital until I talked to the doctor operating on Steve, so I called my sister, Margie, and asked her if she would mind getting the kids for me on her way home from work.

When it came to Sean and Brittany, I had always tried to be very self-sufficient and rarely asked anyone for help. Even though we were very close, I hated to burden Margie with my problems. She worked and had a family of her own. When she asked me what had happened, I told her the whole story starting with the CAT scan on the previous Friday. I promised that I would call her as soon as I knew how much longer it would be until I could come pick up Sean and Brittany.

At 6:30 p.m., after four hours of waiting, I couldn't stand it any longer. A nurse passed by and I asked if she could please try and find out what was going on and why it was taking so long. She was very understanding and said she would see what she could find out for me. She came right back out and said that they had just finished with the surgery and that they were taking Steve to the cardiac care unit. She assured me that, as soon as they got him stabilized, I would be able to see him for a few minutes. Then she had a volunteer escort me to yet another waiting room.

Finally, a surgeon, who I had never met before, came in to talk to me. I would learn later that he was the same surgeon that had done the bronchoscopy. He said that they had originally intended to just make a small incision to perform a deeper biopsy. However, when they had started the procedure, Steve was unable to tolerate it and they needed to put him on a breathing machine. Because of the problems, it took much longer than they had anticipated and Steve would have to stay for a few days until he stabilized.

As I was waiting to see Steve, I thought of questions I wished I had asked the surgeon before he rushed off. What weren't they telling me? If it was just a deeper biopsy, why did they have to do it so fast? Why couldn't Steve tolerate the procedure? Why had it taken so long? What had really happened in the operating room? Why was he in the CCU instead of the ICU? Was there something wrong with his heart?

I wanted to burst through the doors of the CCU and demand answers. Luckily, just then, my brother, Bob, and his wife, Pat, walked into the waiting room. Margie had called them and asked them to come over to stay with me. I was both grateful and surprised to see them. I appreciated their concern and support, but I thought it odd that anyone — Margie, Bob or Pat — felt that they needed to be there with me. I was fine and Steve was just having another biopsy done. Why was everyone making such a big deal out of this?

What seemed like an eternity passed before someone finally called me on the white wall phone in the waiting room. I was allowed to see Steve for just a few minutes, but he was still heavily sedated and probably didn't even know I was there.

As I walked into the CCU, I was completely unprepared for what I saw. Steve was lying with tubes coming out of every part of his body. He was hooked up to all sorts of machines, which were monitoring his vital signs. His face was so pale and he looked helpless. He was still and seemed lifeless. It was like a scene from a movie. I had never been so terrified in my entire life and I felt as though I would faint. My heart was racing and my hands were sweating and, for just a moment, I let myself think the unthinkable. What if he didn't make it through this? What would I do?

I quickly pulled myself together. I refused to let myself think like that. After all, this was a hospital. He couldn't be in a safer place. Everything would be just fine.

I leaned over the side rail and spoke to him softly. I told him I was there and that I loved him and that everything was going to be fine. I wasn't even sure that he could hear me, but I wanted him to know I was with him just in case. The nurse said that he was still heavily sedated and reminded me that I could only stay a moment. I moved my hand away from Steve's, kissed him gently on the cheek, asked the nurse a few questions that she couldn't answer and reluctantly turned to leave.

As I walked towards the door, my eyes filled with tears and I felt my knees shake. I wasn't sure that I would be able to make it to the parking lot without collapsing. Bob and Pat may have been with me the entire time, but I felt very alone.

It was beginning to get dark. As the cold, damp air hit my face, I was returned to reality and felt an urgency to get to Margie's house to pick up Sean and Brittany. I was sure she had fed them, but they would have homework to do and baths to take and they were probably getting tired.

As I drove down the long stretch of expressway, I realized for the first time in a very long time how much I depended on Steve for my strength. I felt so afraid and alone and helpless. As we rushed through our busy days together worrying about all the little unimportant details of life, it had become easy to forget what was really important. I knew as never before how deeply I loved the man I had just left and how empty my life would be should anything ever happen to take him away from me. I promised that I would work harder at letting him know how much I loved and appreciated him and how important he was to me.

As I pulled into Margie's driveway, I realized that I had been crying. Tears ran down my red, swollen face and my nose was running. I tried to pull myself together and put on my "everything is just fine" face. I didn't want the kids to be worried or think something was wrong. I really didn't know yet how serious Steve's condition was and there was no sense in getting everyone upset needlessly.

My mind raced all night and I couldn't sleep because I was so worried. I could hardly wait until I could get back to the hospital the next morning to find out how Steve was doing. I knew that days began early at hospitals so I got up early and took the kids to a neighbor's house to wait for their bus. I was relieved to find him awake, looking much better and wondering why I hadn't been there when he came out of surgery the day before. It was so wonderful to hear his voice. I kissed him and assured him that I had been there, but he had been too out of it to remember.

I asked him if any of the doctors had been by to see him yet. Had anyone explained to him why they were in such a hurry the day before when they took him down for surgery? One of his nurses overheard us and said that the doctors would begin their rounds at any moment. I needed answers to my questions and didn't want to leave until we had talked to someone who knew what was going on and could tell us what we were up against.

Steve knew how I felt about Dr. Keller and how angry I was at him and, in an effort to avoid any embarrassment, asked me to please not start anything with him if he came by while I was there. We had hardly finished our conversation when then the doors of the CCU opened and in walked Dr. Keller.

He spent several minutes looking over Steve's chart and talking to the nurses and then he came over and said good morning. He told us that he had some very good news. The biopsies were back and it **definitely wasn't cancer.**

He explained that Steve would have to stay in the hospital for a few days until they identified the virus that was causing his breathing difficulties and developed a treatment plan. He went on to say that Steve would probably require at least two years of treatment before he returned to normal, but that, fortunately, our lungs are capable of repairing themselves over time and the outlook was extremely encouraging.

We both cried tears of relief and thanked him for letting us know. I had gone through a bout with breast cancer just a few years earlier and, even though we hadn't actually talked about it to each other during the past week, somewhere in the back of both of our minds laid that terrible fear that it might be cancer.

I stayed a little longer and then I told Steve to try and get some rest and that I would come back to see him on my lunch hour. I told everyone at work the good news about the results of the biopsy and the great relief that I felt. A tremendous weight had been lifted from me.

When I got back to the hospital at lunch, Steve's mother and his sister, Lynn, were there and he was sitting up in his chair eating lunch. He was a wonderful storyteller and he was telling them how great his epidural was and how he was sure he could have a baby if he got to use one of these remarkable devices. He said he was never going to have it taken out and wanted me to ask the nurse if he could take it home with him.

It was so good to see him getting back to his old self again. He was always making people laugh and I saw this as a sign that he was doing much better. He was still very weak and pale, but I truly felt the worst was over. At least, it wasn't cancer and we would soon have the answers to all of our questions.

Steve had already won the hearts of the nurses and one of them stopped by his bed to see how he was doing and told us that they were going to be moving him to the step-down unit later in the afternoon. I went back to work assuring him that I would be back later with Sean and Brittany.

I picked the kids up from their after-school daycare at 5:30 p.m. and, when I told them we were going to the hospital to see Steve, Sean said he didn't want to go. My father had died a long, horrible death just the year before and Sean had been very close to him. It was hard for him to watch as this magical man he adored slowly lost the battle against this terrible unknown enemy called cancer. I can still see Sean standing in front of my dad's casket with Steve's hands on his shoulders crying so hard that he could hardly breathe.

The death of his grandfather had left Sean confused and emotionally shaken. It didn't surprise me that he was afraid Steve was going to die and that he begged me not to make him go with us to the hospital. I assured him that the doctor had told us that it wasn't cancer. I told him that Dr. Keller had told us just that morning that Steve only had a virus and as soon as they figured out what kind of virus it was, they would let him come home. He would probably be sick for a little bit longer, but that he certainly wasn't going to die. I must have sounded convincing because, reluctantly, he accompanied Brittany and me to see Steve at the hospital. His little hand clutched mine tightly as we walked through the sliding automatic doors.

Steve was still in the CCU, but his nurses, who were wonderfully supportive and professional throughout this whole terrible ordeal, assured me that it was only because there wasn't a room available in the step-down unit yet.

Since he was in a bed on the end, way over in the corner, they let Sean and Brittany go in to see him and we sat with him as he ate his supper. We hadn't eaten yet so they helped him eat his food, leaving nothing on the plate except a rubbery, pink, pickled egg. They asked him a million questions about the surgery and the tubes and the machines, but, most of all, they wanted to know when he would be coming home. It had been a long week of being shuttled here and there and they missed him terribly and wanted things to be back to normal.

We only stayed for a half an hour because we didn't want to disturb the other patients in the CCU. There was no school the next day so Steve told me not to come in so early in the morning. He wanted me to let the kids sleep in and hoped that maybe, by the time we got there, he would be in the step-down unit and we could stay and visit a little bit longer.

13

We all kissed and hugged him goodbye and told him how much we loved him and that we missed him and couldn't wait for him to come home on Saturday. He really was feeling much better and he even asked me to call work and have someone bring a few files to the hospital so he could look over some figures for a client. He was concerned that he had been off work for a whole week and it was a very busy time of year.

I left the hospital feeling very comfortable and hopeful about Steve's prognosis.

As planned, the three of us, bearing gifts and glad tidings, arrived at the hospital at 11:30 the next morning. I couldn't believe it was Friday already. Could a whole week have really passed since this horrible nightmare had begun?

I was surprised to find out that Steve was still in the CCU. They still didn't have a bed available for him in the step-down unit, but the nurse assured me that they would be moving him shortly after lunch.

They had taken out his epidural and the tube in his side. All that was left of all the tubes and wires and contraptions he had been hooked up to was a small oxygen tube around his nose and some heart monitor patches attached to his chest. Clearly, he was in pain. His rosy skin of the day before was now chalky gray. Our entire conversation was strained and I could tell he was trying very hard to pretend everything was okay so that Sean wouldn't worry.

While Steve was busy with the kids, I asked the nurse why he seemed to be getting worse instead of better. She explained that they were trying to wean him from his pain medication. It wasn't unusual, she said, for it to appear that he was worse than the night before because he was no longer on the constant heavy-duty pain medicine. She assured me that they were doing everything they could to make him comfortable.

Steve was complaining that his incision was hurting him and he was clammy and nervous and agitated. He asked if I would take Sean and Brittany home and come back alone to spend the afternoon with him.

There was a definite change in his disposition from the night before, but I attributed it to him being off the epidural and, once again, asked the nurse to try and keep him comfortable until I got back.

Despite his pain, he asked Brittany if he could have a kiss good-bye and leaned over and gently kissed her cheek. He brushed the top of Sean's head with his hand and said, "See ya' tomorrow, buddy."

It was almost 1:30 in the afternoon when I returned to the hospital and Steve had finally been moved to the step-down unit. The move from one unit to another meant a new group of nurses, who were not as familiar with Steve's case. Steve said that he hadn't seen any of his doctors all day and that he wanted me to find out why.

He was in an extremely agitated state and was pacing up and down from the bed to the window. He kept rubbing his right rib cage below the incision. I persuaded him to get back in bed and got a cold wash rag and put it on his forehead to try to calm him down.

He didn't care what the orders were. He wanted me to ask the nurse if he could have something stronger for the terrible pain he was having in his side. They were giving him Percodan every two hours, but it didn't seem like it was helping much. His gown was

15

open and I could see where he had rubbed the bandages loose. I looked at the large horseshoe-shaped incision under his right arm and saw that he had torn some of the stitches loose. I asked the nurse to change the bandages. When I asked her about the pain medication, she asked if Steve had a low tolerance for pain. I had never known him to react like this to pain, but I told her that it was possible.

I still feel guilty about that conversation. Like many wives, I thought most men were big babies who couldn't take much pain. I had no idea what terrible pain Steve was in then or had been in for so long. I wouldn't find out what a truly brave and courageous person he was until much later the next day.

Throughout the afternoon, he dozed off for a few minutes and I was hopeful that he would be able to get some rest, but he would immediately wake up saying that he couldn't get comfortable no matter what position he was in — standing, sitting or laying down. He was still having some trouble breathing, but he couldn't keep the oxygen tube in his nose because he was so nervous. He would take it out and I would put it back in. He snapped at me several times, which was not at all like him.

There was a spot right below his right rib cage where, for many years, he had always gotten what we had thought was a muscle cramp. Over the years I had rubbed that spot for him many times. When he asked me to rub his side, I knew right where he meant. I rubbed and rubbed all afternoon until I thought my fingers would fall off, but nothing seemed to relieve his pain. I believe now that it was probably his liver because the medical records indicated that there was a large mass in his hepatic lobe.

It was late afternoon and the shifts changed again and I asked the new nurse if Steve could have some Flexeril, which is the muscle relaxant that Dr. Keller had prescribed for him over the years for the pain in his right side. The nurse asked me what dosage he usually took and I said I wasn't positive, but that I thought it was 10 mg. I suggested that they might want to call Dr. Keller to find out for sure. When the nurse finally returned with the Flexeril, she informed me that they couldn't reach Dr. Keller or anyone else from his office so they were just going to give him 10 mg.

At around 6:00 that same night, Steve's sister, Lynn, and her husband, Dave, and their little boy, Dino, stopped by with Steve's brother, Dennis, who had driven down from Toledo to see him. Steve tried to make polite conversation, but it was very obvious that he was in far too much pain to make small talk and pretend that everything was okay. His entire body was clammy and I asked the nurse for a new gown and tried to give him a sponge bath. His nerves were like an over-tightened guitar string ready to snap at any moment and he told me to just stop fussing with him. Lynn rubbed his right shoulder blade for over an hour trying to help him relax, but nothing seemed to help.

Finally, at 8:00, everyone left and I hoped that he might be able to settle down and get some sleep.

By 8:30, I felt completely helpless and frustrated. I begged the nurse to give him something stronger for the pain. She checked with pain management, who approved a shot of morphine. Steve seemed to calm down a bit after the shot and I told him that I was going to leave, thinking that he might be able to fall asleep more easily if I wasn't there bothering him. I needed to pick Sean and Brittany up from Kym's house anyway.

Just as I was about to walk out the door he said, "Please don't go, Kathy. Can't you call Kym and say you're staying a little longer? I don't want to be alone. I'm so scared." I asked him what it was that he was scared about and he said he didn't know for sure. He said, "Please just crawl up here on the bed with me and hold me until I fall asleep." I expressed my concern that one of the nurses might walk in and find us and he said, "You don't have to get naked. Just lay here and hold me." We both laughed as I crawled up next to him and gently laid my arm across his chest.

I held him until he fell asleep and then I quietly slipped out of the room. **No kiss!** I was afraid that I might wake him. I turned and looked back over my shoulder at him lying there and thought how thankful I was that he was resting at last and how much I loved him.

I stopped by the nurses' desk outside his room and told them that they should call me if he needed me and that I would be there no matter what time it was — even if he just said my name or asked for me.

I have relived those last moments at the hospital over and over again in my mind hundreds of thousands of times trying to remember every single detail of what we said and did. I have felt many emotions — among them: pain, sorrow, guilt, anger and regret. No matter how many times I go over it, nothing changes. It was our last few moments together and I would gladly give my own life to have the opportunity to do it differently. If only I had stayed.

I left the hospital parking deck exhausted. It had been a very long day and it wasn't over yet. I had to pick up Sean and Brittany and attempt to catch up on all the things around the house that I had been neglecting. I had been at the hospital so much all week that I hadn't even opened the mail.

I finally climbed into bed at around 11:30 p.m., my mind spinning with the events of the past few days. The overwhelming feeling of emptiness in the bed next to me was unbearable. I put on Steve's robe and breathed deeply from his pillow.

I'm not sure when I dozed off, but I woke up to the sound of Steve's voice calling out to me. "**Kathy.**" It was 1:30 a.m. and I was alone, but it was definitely his voice. I tried to convince myself that I was just dreaming, but it sounded like he was right there next to me.

I almost went to the phone and called the hospital, but the phone at the nurses station was right outside his room and I didn't want anything to disturb him if he were, by some chance, still asleep. The nurses had assured me that they would call me if he needed me.

I turned on the television hoping it would help put me back to sleep, but my mind kept going back to hearing Steve's voice and I continued to struggle about whether or not I should call the hospital. I must have fallen back to sleep because the next thing I remember is answering the phone. "**Mrs. Donatini, this is the hospital calling. I'm afraid your husband, Steve, has taken a turn for the worse and we feel you should get here as soon as possible.**"

I somehow found myself walking up to Steve's bed. The drive, parking, the elevator, everything slid away when I saw him. He was again hooked up to a mass of tubes and wires and mechanical devices. His eyes were shut and he was so still and when I touched his hand it was cold, so very, very cold.

I said, "Baby, I'm here. It's me, Kathy. I'm here now and everything is going to be okay." He couldn't answer me. I'd gotten there too late. It had only been a half an hour since they called me, but I was too late. Oh, if only I'd stayed. Why hadn't I stayed with him? He needed me and I was at home sleeping.

The nurses said that his blood pressure had dropped too low and his heart stopped and he had stopped breathing. Steve had coded at 1:30 a.m. at exactly the same time I had woken — **Kathy** — and heard him call out to me. They were able to stabilize him, but he needed the tubes and the machines to keep him alive.

They were sure that he could hear us speaking. They had paralyzed him somehow from the chest down so that he wouldn't have to be strapped down because he had been thrashing around.

At that point, I truly had no idea that he had no chance for survival. If I stayed right beside him and talked to him and comforted him, I was sure that one of his doctors would arrive and tell the rest of the staff what to do to correct the problem and everything would be okay.

This was just a crisis. Surely, he couldn't be dying. This was Saturday morning. This was the day I was going to come get him and bring him home.

The truth was — God had come to take him "Home" long before I even got there. His spirit may have still been there in the room somewhere to make sure that we were all okay, but his physical life on Earth was over.

They all started to arrive: my brothers and their wives, Margie's husband, Steve's mother and brother, his sister and her husband. Had I called them or had someone else? Why are they here? Steve has a virus and he is coming home today.

It was all like a bad dream. Nothing seemed real and it felt as if everything was moving in slow motion. I would slip in and out of reality.

Someone asked me to make a decision about whether or not I wanted to keep him alive. Where had my voice gone? I shouted in my mind, "Of course, I want him alive." Had they all lost their minds?

Please, somebody help me! I don't understand what's happening. Oh, God, please help me. I can't breathe.

I kept thinking that I was dreaming and that I would wake up and find myself back in my own bed and that this would all be just a horrible nightmare.

I would be at his bed and then all of a sudden I'd find myself back in the waiting room talking to someone. Confused about how I had gotten there, I would again wander back to his bed.

There were so many people around his bed working on him. Why couldn't someone tell me what was going on? Where were his doctors?

At some point, someone asked me if I wanted to call a priest — Oh, God, they want to give him his last rights.

HELP ME, PLEASE SOMEONE HELP ME! MY HUSBAND IS DYING AND I DON'T KNOW WHAT TO DO.

I had no concept of time. At some point, I was taken to a room where yet another doctor that I had never seen before told me that Steve's biopsy reports were back.

This doctor said that Steve had terminal lung cancer and, even in the unlikely event that Steve could be kept alive throughout the day, he would probably only live two weeks to two months longer.

He would undoubtedly suffer terribly. The cancer was too advanced and there was no treatment available that would save him. I was being asked to give my permission to stop all lifesaving efforts and let him die naturally.

What seemed like only seconds later, I found myself standing outside the hospital with Margie. I wanted to run far and fast, away from the hospital and the doctors and the lung cancer and everything that was happening. I was no runner, but the urge was overwhelming.

The pain was so intense that I was sure that I would explode if I didn't scream. When I started screaming, it was almost primal. A man whose name I didn't even know had just told me that the man whose name I shared was going to die. If not today, tomorrow. If not tomorrow, soon. This can't be happening. My mind returned again to the thought that Steve just had a bad cough, to the notion that this was just a bad dream. I desperately willed myself awake.

Just two days earlier, Dr. Keller had told us that the biopsies had come back negative and that Steve didn't have cancer. Were these the same biopsies this new doctor was talking about? Surely, they were mistaken. They must have picked up the wrong chart.

Where was Dr. Keller? He'd tell them that Steve didn't have cancer and then we could get this whole thing straightened out. Where was the pulmonary specialist? I wanted to talk to someone I knew, not some intern or this doctor, whoever he was. Where was everyone? Why weren't they telling me what had really happened?

I would find out much later that the biopsy that Dr. Keller had read the previous Thursday and so cheerfully informed us was negative was from the bronchoscopy that was done on Tuesday. The Prednisone Steve had been given for so long by Dr. Keller had caused a false negative reading. The second biopsy was done to get deeper tissue to obtain more accurate results.

If only someone had been honest with us and told us that they suspected cancer and that they wouldn't know until early Saturday morning what we were really dealing with, we would have had time to talk to each other about what we were feeling. We could have comforted each other and held each other and said "I love you." I could have talked to Sean and Brittany and tried to explain that it might be cancer. At the very least, it wouldn't have been such a shock.

Most of all, I would have never left Steve's side for one moment. I would have been there every second of every hour of every day for the entire week for whatever time was left. How wrong they were to have taken that away from us. What right did they have to keep us in the dark.

I had just closed the book I was reading and turned off the light on the table next to the bed when I heard the garage door open and Steve's car pull into the garage. It was a little later than he usually got home, but it was tax season and sometimes he stayed late so he could work without interruption.

He seemed surprised to find me in bed so early and asked, "You okay?" I'd had breast cancer surgery in January and had gone in for my chemo the day before. The first few days after each treatment were always the worst and left me running on empty by the end of the day.

"I'm fine, just a little tired. I got the kids down early and decided to crawl in early myself."

"I had lunch with Bob today." he said, dropping his clothes to the floor. Bob was a long-time friend of his whose wife was fighting what was beginning to look like a hopeless battle against cancer. "Things aren't going so well. I wish there were more I could do for him. He's so exhausted. I really admire him. I don't think I could do it." He lay down next to me and wrapped his arms around my waist, his muscles willing me to survive.

"You could, if you had to, we both could." The room resonated with our unspoken words until I said, "Unless there was no chance of recovery. Promise me you'll let me go, if it comes to that."

"I promise. Same goes for me. Promise."

"Promise."

Just a small five-minute conversation that had taken place over four years earlier that would make the next few minutes a little less painful.

One of the doctors called the immediate family to Steve's bedside and talked about the gravity of Steve's condition and tried to make us understand that there was absolutely no hope for any type of recovery. If they unhooked him from the life support now or tomorrow or the next day, the result would be the same. It was doubtful that he could survive on his own and he would certainly not live longer than a few more days or weeks no matter what we decided to do. Even though they were still getting signs that he was aware of his surroundings, he definitely would never regain consciousness and be able to talk to us.

A priest from our parish came in to give Steve his last rights and afterwards we all took turns being alone with him for a few moments. As I stood beside his bed holding his motionless hand in mine, the certainty of his death flooded over me.

At 11:25 a.m., after talking to his family, I signed some papers giving the doctors permission to shut off the life support systems. The hospital records would show that I only wanted them to maintain comfort levels, but that must be the medical terminology. I don't really remember saying anything at all. I just remember looking up at the clock to see what time it was.

It's strange the multitude of thoughts that rush through your mind in those last moments. Things you want him to know, things you might have forgotten to say, things you said and wish you could take back, things you did and wished you hadn't, things you didn't do and wished you had, things - so many things. I'll love you forever. I'm so proud to be your wife. I'm sorry I didn't do more to help you. I didn't mean to hurt you. I wish I'd stayed instead of going home. Forgive me!

But, most of all I remember not wanting to let go and watching as his blood pressure slowly dropped notch by notch and thinking, **"No, please don't take him yet. I made a mistake. Hook him back up! Give me just one moment longer. Please, God, please I can't bear to lose him yet. It hurts too much. I can't do this. I'm not ready yet."**

And then, at 11:45 a.m. on Saturday, March 14, 1998, Steve took his last breath and was pronounced officially dead.

I heard moaning. It took a moment to realize that it was me. I was having difficulty breathing and the sound of my heartbeat was so loud inside my head that I thought my eardrums would burst.

The pain in my chest was unbearable. Surely, someone's hand had reached into my chest and grabbed hold of my heart and was trying to stop it from beating. I felt lightheaded and disoriented. I gasped for breath. I didn't have the strength to fight it. It would have been easier to bear if my heart had simply been ripped out, if the life were just taken from me. I had no need for it now.

That feeling is still with me today. I carry it in my heart. It may not be quite as severe, but it is still here inside my chest. You learn to live with it. Just when you think it might be gone for good, something happens to bring it all rushing back. A song, a smell, a place, a memory ....

They gave me a moment and then I remember shouting at someone "Would somebody get these damn tubes and wires and shit off of him?" Those poor nurses. They had been so kind and wonderful and here I was yelling at them. I went back the next week to thank them and apologize for my impatience. It wasn't their fault, but they took the brunt of my anger.

I just wanted to get up on the bed and lie down next to him and hold him in my arms and never let him go. I remember saying something about not wanting them to hurt him and could they please be more careful.

Steve's brother, Dennis' voice came from somewhere behind me trying to assure me that he couldn't feel anything they were doing. I just wanted to turn around and slap him.

I had always prided myself on how I was able to control everything and all of a sudden I couldn't control anything.

Shut up, just shut up! This is my husband. What do you know about what he can or cannot feel? Damn you all! My life is falling apart right here in front of me and I can't stop it. Just shut up and leave me alone!

They finally finished unhooking everything and everyone slowly disappeared, leaving me alone with Steve to say my goodbyes.

Steve had a large blue bruise on his upper lip where the oxygen tube had been and I licked my thumb and tried to rub it off as if it were a smudge of dirt. His skin felt strange beneath my fingertips, cold and rubbery. Everything had changed so quickly. One moment he was alive and the next moment he was gone and all that was left was this lifeless body.

I pulled the sheet back so that I could look one last time at the body that I had grown to know so well over the past 20 years. There wasn't an inch that I hadn't touched. I tried to memorize it so that I wouldn't forget a single part: his skinny, little, bony Donatini legs; his fingernails that grew so fast and that he took such care of; his beautiful, dark, shiny hair that I had loved to run my fingers through; the scar on his forehead from a car accident he'd had before I met him; that one hair in his eyebrow that always grew too long and I used to cut for him; the mole on his cheek that he hated; the spot in the middle of the back of his neck that I would massage when he had a headache; his strong, muscular chest that I'd laid my head on so many times at night and his soft, sweet lips that I had kissed ten million times.

As I lay there beside him I knew that it would be the last time I would be able to hold him and I never wanted to let go. The world could have ended at that moment and it would have been just fine with me.

Someone's voice in the background said that the funeral home was there for the body. I have no idea who was talking or to whom they were talking. I didn't even remember discussing whether or not to call them and they were there already. How could they have gotten there so quickly? Had someone called them before he'd died? How much time had passed? What time was it?

Someone asked me if I wanted them to perform an autopsy. I know now that Steve's spirit was no longer connected to his body and that he couldn't feel anything, but, at that moment — looking at Steve's lifeless body — I didn't want anyone else poking at him or cutting him or even touching him. I just wanted them to leave him alone so he could be at peace. I was so angry and confused and I just wanted to hit someone.

I wish they'd have waited to ask me later on in the day when I was less emotional or that they'd have asked another member of our family to talk to me about it. It was a decision that couldn't be reversed and I will regret it forever. I was once again working under the misconception that the doctors knew what they were doing and that they would be able to tell me what had happened. I couldn't have been more wrong!

I may never know all the details of what actually went on that week that no one would discuss with me. No one could give me an answer. I didn't know it then, but they actually knew a lot more than they were willing to admit. Try as I might, I was unable to get any of the doctors involved to go out on a limb and tell me what they really thought. The risk was too great. Protecting each other ranked way up there above protecting the rights of the patient or his family.

I could've accepted that he had incurable lung cancer, but I just couldn't figure out why he died so suddenly or how he got lung cancer in the first place when he never even smoked. Doctors I talked to later, who weren't there that night, came up with several probabilities. Maybe he had thrown a blood clot, maybe he'd had something called sarcoidosis, maybe he'd had liver cancer that had spread to his lungs or maybe it was shock brought on by improper weaning from his Prednisone prior to surgery.

I am certain of one thing. You'll rarely get a doctor to tell you the truth about something if they think it might mean they would have to admit they made a mistake or that it might cost them money and, even if you might be able to prove it, they will still never admit you are right.

I didn't want to be right. I just wanted to know the truth. It wasn't about right or wrong. It was about finding peace. If they'd only known how much it would've helped to ease the pain. The not knowing was the hardest part.

As I walked into the waiting room, I looked up and saw the faces of the people around me and I realized that this was not just my tragedy. Everyone there loved Steve or me or Sean or Brittany or someone else in the room so much that they came rushing to the hospital in the middle of the night just to comfort us, to comfort one another. We were truly blessed, but I didn't feel it at that moment. It would be months or years before I would begin to connect the word "blessing" to Steve's death.

Steve's mother sat in a chair by herself staring down at her hands. She'd lost a child before — Dean, who had died at a very young age before Steve was even born. I can't imagine the pain she must have felt. She'd lost her husband suddenly and now she was losing Steve. If my pain was unbearable, what must hers be? I wanted to put my arms around her, but I didn't. In the years that I had known her, she had always seemed uncomfortable with hugging.

I searched for Margie and felt foolish when I realized that she was standing right beside me gently holding my elbow. She was five years younger than me and, as children, we hadn't been as close as some sisters, but that changed as we became adults. She is my best friend in the world. I didn't have to try and understand how she was feeling. We always just seem to know. Sometimes it is as if we are the same person in different bodies.

Steve's sister, Lynn, was sitting with her husband. She looked tired and her face was swollen from crying. She had a cell phone in her hand and I could tell that she was trying to retain her composure by keeping busy organizing what she had to do next. I hugged her, but I don't think she understood that I was trying to comfort her. Perhaps, she wasn't thinking of her own pain yet.

Three of my brothers were there with their wives. Scott, who wasn't there, lived out of town and someone had mentioned that he and his family were on their way. I could tell by the way they stood holding one another's hands and by their haunted eyes that the shock of Steve's death had made them think about their own relationships and about how fragile life truly was. Their support was so comforting to me and I could tell they wished they could do more. I felt momentarily ashamed. Only a few nights earlier, I had arrogantly thought that I didn't need anyone. I needed them more than I could express and, as always, they were all there.

Steve's brother, Dennis, was talking to someone I didn't know. Dennis looked very calm and composed. I thought it was odd that he wasn't crying. Maybe he felt he had to remain in control. Maybe he needed his wife, Chris, who was on her way to the hospital, to be there to comfort him before he could let his guard down. He was very supportive over the next few days, going out of his way to be there for me. At the funeral, when I read Steve's eulogy, he stood beside me and supported me so I wouldn't collapse. He never said a word to me about how he had felt. Perhaps losing his younger brother made him stop and think about his own mortality. Maybe it was more than he could bear and he decided that pretending it wasn't happening might help him deal with it better. I'll probably never know. To this day, we have not spoken of our loss with one another, but that's okay because everyone should be entitled to the privacy of their own grief.

My daughter, Kym, was sitting on a couch talking to my brother Craig's wife, Phyllis. Kym had been eight years old when Steve and I were married and Steve adopted her shortly thereafter. I'd spoiled her terribly and over the years she and Steve had fought about everything. There were unresolved issues that she would eventually have to deal with, but she seemed to be holding up fairly well considering the circumstances. I reminded myself to make some time for her when we got home.

I had called one of Steve's closest friends, Linda, after I got to the hospital. They had worked together for 23 years and had a very special relationship. They were best friends. Steve loved her and she loved him. There had been gossip over the years and I knew that people suspected that they were having an affair. I never asked Steve if it was true. I didn't believe it and I didn't care what people thought. I'm sure there were people who speculated again when they heard she had been at the hospital that night, but it was not as important to me as Linda's opportunity to say goodbye. She had been part of Steve's life for a long time and I know if the shoe had been on the other foot, she would have called me to come and say goodbye to him. She was my friend too and I needed her to be there. Her loss was profound and she has helped me through many rough times over the past few years. It's nice to have someone to talk to who knew Steve nearly as well as I did. We share a wonderful bond of friendship through our love of the same man.

Linda was in the hallway talking to a mutual friend of theirs, Jim, who had actually worked with Steve at his old bank and followed him when he left and went to his new job only a few months earlier. Jim and Steve made a great team and had many grand plans for the years ahead of them. I had just spoken to him a few days earlier and asked him to bring Steve the files he wanted. He had just come to visit and walked in only moments after Steve had died. As I watched Jim and Linda cry in each others arms, it was obvious that their pain was genuine. They had both just lost a dear friend and their lives would be drastically changed, both personally and professionally. They have since helped me sort through all the legal and financial details that come with death and I feel blessed to have them as my friends.

Just then, out of the corner of my eye, I saw a gurney coming down the hall carrying a dark bag. I thought, "Oh, my God, that can't possibly be Steve." If it was, surely there must have been another way they could have taken the gurney. Did they think we were already gone? It was unbelievably painful to watch. What a harsh reality.

Steve was really gone. His body was in that bag on that gurney heading for the funeral home. I wasn't going to wake up and make it all go away. It wasn't a dream. They might just have well been taking me too because I didn't want to go on without him.

Before leaving the hospital, I went to the step-down unit and asked the nurse for Steve's personal belongings. His jacket, shoes and other clothes were in a locker when I had left the night before and I realized that he hadn't had his glasses on since I'd arrived earlier that morning.

I'll never forget the pain I felt when they handed his clothes to me. Everything was stuffed in a crumpled-up, brown grocery bag. I asked the nurse if she knew where his glasses were and she said there was a pair at the nurses' station and asked me if I wanted her to go see if they were his. When she brought them back, I took them and thanked her. They were brand new. He had just picked them up a few weeks earlier. I remember telling him how handsome he looked in them.

As I started to walk away, she said, "Mrs. Donatini, do you want his flowers?" I don't think I even bothered to answer her. There would be plenty of flowers sooner than I wanted to think about.

I found myself standing in the driveway of our home. I don't know how I had gotten there, who drove me or even who else was in the car. Someone must have driven my car home from the hospital because I noticed it in the driveway later that day. How did they get my keys? I read somewhere that it is normal for there to be gaps in one's memory during the first few days following the loss of a loved one.

An alarm went off in my head. **Sean! Oh, God, Sean! What would I say to Sean and Brittany**?

I opened the door and saw their worried questioning eyes looking up at me. "Where was Daddy? Wasn't he supposed to be coming home today? Why are you crying? Why are all these people here?"

Kym and I led them upstairs to my bedroom so we could have some privacy while we talked to them. Sean started crying immediately. He already knew. I didn't have to tell him. Steve wasn't coming home. He was dead! I could see the anger rise up in his tear-stained face. I tried to comfort him, but he stiffened and turned

33

to Kym. He looked up at me and said, "I told you he was going to die, but you wouldn't listen to me."

Brittany, who is very different emotionally from Sean, was very quiet and seemed as though she didn't quite fully understand. Her eyes teared up and she let me comfort her for a moment and then she wanted to know if she could go downstairs and see who was there. I would find out later that summer when she attended a special camp for kids who had lost a close loved one, that the impact on her was much more profound than I had realized at that moment. She understood much more than I did about life and dying. She still does!

Sean was only nine years old and Brittany only eight and already they had learned a hard lesson about trust. It was a long time before I could tell either of them something without them questioning whether or not I was telling them the truth. They didn't trust me anymore and I didn't blame them. Dr. Keller's mistake would be a dark cloud that would hang over our heads for years.

I was twenty years old and pregnant when I got married the first time. Bill and I had only been dating for a year. Our wedding was in June of 1968 and Kym was born in January of 1969. I was divorced in March. In total, Bill and I hadn't even been married for a year and we only lived together for a few months.

After the divorce, Kym and I moved back into my parents home. I went to work every day and, with the help of my parents, I was able to provide for the two of us. There were many days when it was overwhelming. I was so young and so unprepared to raise a child. I loved my little girl very much, perhaps too much. She was an adorable, blonde-haired, blue-eyed child. Everywhere we went people commented on how beautiful she was. My parents loved her like grandparents love their grandchildren and my brothers treated her like a little sister. She seldom asked for something she didn't immediately receive from one or the other of us. We set her up to become overindulged and spoiled.

My ex-husband was never involved in Kym's life and he never paid me child support. I was trained as a secretary and had no trouble earning a paycheck. The only problem was that it wasn't enough to pay for daycare, an apartment, utilities, food, car insurance and all the other things that go along with living on your own with a newborn baby. I didn't earn enough to support us and I earned too much to collect welfare. It didn't matter anyway because my father wouldn't have stood for it. He was a very proud man and was from a generation that had very strong opinions about the type of people who collected public assistance.

Our living arrangement wasn't easy on anyone involved. My mother and I didn't get along well under normal circumstances and here we were living together under one roof. Somehow we all managed to survive living together for the first six years of Kym's life. I am sure that my entire family was thrilled beyond words when I could finally afford to move out.

On occasion, my dad still helped me out when my car would break down or I needed something fixed. Every once in a while, he would show up at my front door unexpectedly with a couple of bags of groceries. There were even occasions when my parents would baby sit so I could go out.

When Kym was 7 years old, I met Steve and we were married the next year. I felt so lucky to have found someone I loved, someone who actually seemed to love me back and was willing to take on responsibility for another man's child. Steve adopted Kym six months after our wedding day and I was sure we would become one big happy family.

Unfortunately, neither of them ever saw it that way. It was a struggle from the start for the two of them. We went to counseling, I read books, we tried everything we could think of, but nothing seemed to work. Kym was used to getting her own way and Steve had very different ideas about parenting than I did. He set the bar so much higher than I had that I'm sure Kym must have felt that she would never be able to be what he wanted her to be. The little strides that she made went unnoticed because they weren't even close to what he expected from her. At some point, she just stopped trying to impress him and they both just accepted their relationship for what it was.

Kym dropped out of high school three months before graduation. By the time she was 20, she was unhappily married and had two children — Sean and Brittany — within almost a year of one another. Neither she nor her husband, Tom, were working and they received public assistance. If we hadn't helped them out financially, it would have been next to impossible for them to pay their bills.

At first, Steve and I would pick up Sean and Brittany on our way home from work on Fridays and drop them back off on Monday. Eventually, we were picking them up on Wednesday nights as well and keeping them overnight. This went on for around six or eight months. Each weekend, I struggled with my concern for their well being and my fear of doing too much. I finally spoke to Steve about bringing the kids to live with us until Kym and Tom could get their lives together. Steve loved Sean and Brittany as if they were his own children and agreed that we should look into what we needed to do legally to bring them home to live with us.

I never felt that they were being abused by Kym or Tom, but I did think they were neglected. The house reeked of cigarette smoke and there were piles of dirty dishes stacked everywhere in the kitchen. Both of the babies would be in wet diapers and dirty undershirts and I would find baby bottles lying around with curdled milk in them. Sean would be strapped in the high chair in front of the television set eating Cheerios or a cut up hotdog and drinking Gatorade and Brittany would be way back in a corner sitting in the day carrier in the playpen all by herself. There were rarely clean clothes so I would take baskets of dirty things to our house to be washed. Kym would be lying on the couch in her nightgown sleeping or watching some mindless television show completely oblivious to the horrid conditions in which they were living.

Kym said that lots of her friends lived like she did and their families didn't seem to think it was so horrible, but it just wasn't how I had been raised. It wasn't how I had raised her either.

Steve never complained about the money or time we spent on Sean and Brittany. They were his grandbabies and he adored them. He was adamant, however, that we not enable Kym and Tom by doing everything for them. He felt that they would never try and improve their lives as long as they had us there supporting them. Despite the fact that I knew he was right, as often as I could, I would give them money behind his back.

"I can't do this any longer," Steve said to me one Friday evening. We had just picked up Sean and Brittany and they were in the backseat. I didn't know what he meant at first. I thought that he was going to turn the car around and take the kids back home. I thought the thing he "couldn't do" was take Sean and Brittany on weekends. "Until I see some major changes, I can't live knowing they have to spend even one more day in that house."

We just didn't take them back the following Monday. I took the week off from work to look for a nursery school and we went to a lawyer. Soon after that, we were given temporary custody of 22-month old Sean and 10-month old Brittany. At the time that Kym signed the custody papers, she was very agreeable and said she understood. I had told her that I was concerned about them not having medical insurance and that we could cover them under ours if we had custody and they lived in our house. I'm sure she had felt that the arrangement was only temporary and that she would soon be able to take them back.

Tom had signed the papers as well, but I found out later that he had been against it. He told Kym that he didn't trust Steve and was afraid they would never be able to get them back. He felt he wouldn't stand a chance should a legal battle ensue. She manipulated him into signing, all the time assuring him that we would never try and keep them forever.

The kids always knew that we were their grandparents and that Kym and Tom were their parents. They were both involved in Sean and Brittany's lives on a regular basis in the beginning, but they were very young and had so many problems.

In hindsight, I can see that Kym was probably going through postpartum. She had never really recovered from the first pregnancy before she found herself immediately pregnant again. I had never trained her to take care of herself, let alone a house, husband and two babies. The whole thing must have been overwhelming to her. It is no wonder that she chose to escape into another world through sleep, television and cigarettes.

When you first met Tom, he seemed to be a likeable enough guy. He was unaware that he was doing anything wrong. He came from a background where he was never taught how to function outside the world he had always known. As a child, Tom was difficult for his parents to handle. I suspect that he had some learning disabilities and he struggled in school. He was labeled bad from the start and he never completed grade school.

It was hard for me to try and put myself in his place. He didn't seem to have any sense of the importance of following the rules of society. He thought nothing of driving without a driver's license or not having car insurance or moving out of an apartment and not paying the past due rent or the overdue utility bills. As I look back now, I can see that he had no choice. He was doing the best he could. If he let himself worry about where he would get the money to pay for things, he would have gone crazy trying to keep up.

He worked as a physical laborer for a few months at a time until he would eventually get mad and quit or he would get fired because he couldn't keep up with the day-to-day responsibility of holding down a job. Through no fault of his own, he just didn't have the skills to be more than he was. He could never have been better, he was already the best that he knew how to be.

I don't think Kym was ever really in love with him the way most people think of being in love and I'm sure that she wouldn't have even married him if I hadn't forced the issue when I found out she was pregnant with Sean. She was too young to know that she had other options. She did what we told her to do. She trusted us and we said it would be okay. Then, we took the kids and Tom was what she was left with.

Eventually, they got divorced and both remarried. Tom and his new wife had two kids of their own and, except for maybe an occasional visit at Christmas or Easter or on Sean or Brittany's birthdays, he slipped out of the picture almost entirely. Kym and her new husband, Joe, struggled with their own issues and the time just never seemed right for her to take them back.

At some point, it wouldn't have mattered how well Kym did or who she married. The more Steve loved Sean and Brittany, the more he hated Kym. She didn't stand a chance. I often wished that he had met Kym when she was a baby so that he would have fallen in love with her the way he did Sean and Brittany. We were the adults and she was the child when we first met. It was our responsibility to behave properly and guide her and love her. We had both failed her.

Right or wrong, things turned out as they did. Sean and Brittany were with us and that was just how it was. Looking back, given the chance, I wouldn't have done it differently. As the years went by, Kym often told me that I altered her life by taking them and has blamed many of her personal problems on me. Maybe she is right. I don't know. She says she would have become a better person because she would have had to in order to take care of them by herself.

I can't go back and second guess my decisions. What good would it do. It is just something with which I have learned to live. Sometimes it's not easy doing what you think is right for one person you love knowing that it might hurt another that you love just as much. I had to choose the side where I felt the need was the greatest.

I guess the point I'm trying to make by explaining all of this in such detail was so that you would understand that Sean and Brittany had not only just lost their grandfather. They had also just lost the man who had been their father figure for the past 8 to 9 years. Their safe little world had just been shattered into millions of pieces and I wasn't sure I was going to be able to survive myself, let alone put it back together again for them.

40

God created this magical state of being called "shock" to help us get through times of tremendous loss and devastation. Without this gift, I could have never survived the first three days after Steve's death.

That first afternoon, after I got home from the hospital, there were people coming and going, decisions being made regarding the funeral, food and flowers being delivered and the phone seemed to ring constantly. I truly don't remember much of any of it.

I do, however, remember Margie asking who I wanted her to call and notify of Steve's death. The people I worked with, the people Steve worked with, close neighbors, friends and family who would have to come from out of town and might not see it in the paper. She was, without a doubt, my lifeline throughout those first few terrible days. Without her I don't think I could have remained afloat. I would have just let myself sink down into the whirlpool that was forming around me and never have come back up.

My house was a mess and there was laundry that had piled up over the past week. I was never what you might call Susie Homemaker, but it was even worse than usual. She immediately started straightening things up so that the house would be presentable when people stopped by to see us. She loaded the dishwasher and ran the vacuum and started gathering up loads of laundry to take home with her to wash. When I saw her with it in her arms, I jumped up like a mad woman and grabbed it from her.

Some of those clothes were Steve's and I didn't want her to wash his smell off them. I sorted through them right there on the living room floor in front of everyone and gave the rest back to her. I sat there with those dirty clothes in my lap for the rest of the afternoon. God bless her, she acted as if it was a perfectly rational act and never said a thing.

My brother, Bob, who is two years older than I am, called and wanted to know what he could do. His wife, Pat, works at the cemetery where Steve was to be buried; and, in her normal quiet, low-keyed manner, she went about finding burial plots close to Steve's dad's grave for me.

When my dad passed away, Steve took Sean out to the cemetery so that he could watch them dig the hole for his casket. Sean has always been fascinated with heavy equipment and Steve hoped that it would help prepare him for the funeral. So, when Sean asked me if he could help dig Steve's grave, I said of course and thought nothing of it. I suppose it probably sounds strange to most people, but Sean is truly connected to the earth. He loves to work in the dirt with his hands and he needed to be part of the process. He had been keeping to himself pretty much since the morning he found out and I was just glad there was something in which he wanted to participate.

I will be grateful to Bobby for the rest of my life for taking Sean on this mission of love for his grandfather. I could have never gone; and, although he voiced some concern about how it would go, he reached out to us and helped us when we needed him the most.

I have a group of very close girlfriends who were there for me unconditionally. Some were my best friends in high school, some I had worked with over the years and still others I had met because they were friends of these same friends. I don't have to mention their names. They know who they are. They each came and quietly held me in their arms and comforted me as only someone who has been your friend for many years can. Without their love, I would have crumbled into a heap and never have been able to recover. I am truly blessed to have each of them in my life. When they found out that I was writing this book, we joked and laughed; and they all asked if they could play themselves if, by some chance, it were to be made into a movie. They would have to, because no one else could pretend to be them. They are truly angels living here on Earth.

Everyone from work was wonderful. My boss and his wife were so supportive. They came and brought food and picked up a prescription for me at the drug store and asked what else they could do. During the next few months, their generosity would go far beyond emotional support. They reached out and helped me in ways I had never imagined possible. They are truly compassionate people to whom I will be eternally grateful.

Those first two nights were just the first of many to come when I wouldn't be able to sleep. Someone had called a doctor to get something for me to take and I pretended to take it. There were other people in the house, but I was afraid that Sean or Brittany would need me and I would be too sound asleep and wouldn't hear them.

In the middle of the second night, I started writing Steve a letter. First on paper by hand and then at the computer. I felt as though I hadn't gotten to say goodbye to him and I needed to put something in writing. I worked for hours non-stop on this letter of love.

At some point it became Steve's eulogy, which I read at the funeral service:

In Loving Memory
Stephen C. Donatini
May 13, 1950 to March 14, 1998

I can't tell you how much it means to me that you have all come here today to say goodbye to Steve.

Three days ago my life changed forever. I lost more than just my husband. Steve was my best friend, my soul mate, my lover and my constant companion for over 20 years.

I have been through a lot in my life, but nothing comes near to being as hard as this. The pain I feel is indescribable. But I need to do this as a tribute to Steve because no one knew him better than I did.

When Steve and I decided to get married, we went to Father Dyer and asked him to help us figure out a way for a divorced woman to marry the man she loved in a Catholic church.

We had to jump through a few hoops; but on October 15, 1977, with many of you present, he pronounced us Mr. and Mrs. Stephen C. Donatini at St. John's Catholic Church.

Having Father Dyer here today somehow completes the circle of my precious time as Steve's wife.

Steve used to say to me "Hey, Kathy, do you know what today is?" And, of course, I didn't. Then he would answer something like "It's the anniversary of the first time we kissed or the day we got engaged or the day we moved into our house."

I was never good with dates, but there is one important time that was easy to remember. If you asked me when I knew I loved him, I'd immediately answer "From the moment I laid eyes on him."

When I read his obituary in the paper Sunday, I couldn't help but think how incomplete it was. All the facts were right, but he was so much more than that.

He was my anchor. He kept me grounded. Anything I am today or ever will be is because he loved me.

He supported me when I wanted to get my college degree at age 30, when I got fired from my job at Belden & Blake, when I just had to buy that stupid Volkswagen, and when I brought Sean and Brittany home to live with us.

He loved me when I had braces, when I had cancer, when I was bald and even when I grew old and fat.

He was the most moral person I ever knew. He rarely swore and disliked it when I did. He instilled his faith in Sean and Brittany and taught them right from wrong by his example.

He made people laugh and treated them fair. So many people told me yesterday how much they loved him, depended on him, respected him and would miss him deeply. He was truly held in high esteem by his peers.

He worked at Key Bank for most of his adult life and gave them his all — even when it was almost unbearable. His deep-rooted sense of loyalty caused him to agonize over his decision to leave to join United last year.

He loved his new job and was happy and content. He would come home at night and tell me how he felt he was making a difference and we would talk until late into the night about his plans and ideas.

The doctors said that his cancer was so advanced that they couldn't see how he managed to get out of bed each day let alone put in a full day's work. I truly believe that it was because he loved what he was doing. And for that I thank every one involved with helping me to convince him to change jobs.

I can remember one night in particular when we were at one of the many functions we attended for the bank. We got separated and I looked around to see where he was. As I watched him talking to a group of people, I felt so proud of him. He looked up at me and smiled and I knew I was the luckiest person in the world because he had chosen me for his wife.

Don't get me wrong — It wasn't always sunshine and roses. We fought just like everyone else. We used to joke about the fact that the only reason we had never gotten a divorce was because we never both wanted it at the same time.

He genuinely liked people and made friends easily. Jokes were the name of the game and he loved to play for a crowd. But those to whom he could express his love easily were few. He was too practical to think that anyone needed to hear the words "I love you."

And then along came two little people in the shape of grandchildren and all that love came pouring out. Anyone who knew him could tell you at least one story he had told them about Sean and Brittany. His love for them was endless.

Kym bore the brunt of his "my way or else" parenting years. I can only hope that she realizes that he couldn't have shown her how much he loved her more than by being such a wonderful father to Sean and Brittany.

There were times when he might have been able to leave me, but he could never have survived without them. No biological father could have ever loved his children more than he loved them. Part of him will always live on for me in them.

He wasn't a flower or card or present type of guy. But he showed me he loved me everyday by the little things that I realize now I took all too forgranted.

When he was really in the doghouse, he'd buy me a dark chocolate Milky Way or take me to Bob's Big Boy for lunch.

But when he really wanted to sweep me off my feet, he'd turn on the stereo, and hold me real close and we'd dance real slow to a song by Billy Vera and the Beaters. Somehow he must have known how I'd feel today because the words went something like this:

> *What do you think I would give at this moment?*
> *If you'd stay I'd subtract 20 years from my life.*
> *I'd fall down on my knees.*
> *Kiss the ground that you walk on.*
> *If I could just hold you again.*

I love you, baby. Rest in peace!
Kathy
March 17, 1998

The calling hours were held at Rossi's funeral home and everything was done beautifully. Steve's family had taken care of picking out the coffin and it was just what I would have chosen.

Sean wanted to put Steve's Indians hat in his casket with him and I said, "Of course." He loved that hat. He wore it all the time and I'm sure he would have wanted to take it with him. Brittany asked me if she could put something in with daddy too. I said, "Sure" and waited in anticipation as she ran to her room to retrieve the item, to which she had obviously given a great deal of thought. She came out with her bell and tears filled my eyes.

During Easter break, just the year before, Steve and I had taken the kids to Chicago to get away for a few days. We went to the Sears Tower and to the Shedd Aquarium. Brittany had gotten this gray and blue bell as a souvenir and she and Steve had a little game they would play at night when she would go to sleep. She would say she didn't want him to leave her alone in her bedroom and he would tell her that if she needed him during the night, all she had to do was ring the bell and he would come running. During the last six months of his life, Steve was very sick and was in bed almost all the time. Brittany told him that he should keep the bell in his room for a while. Just until he got better. That way, if he needed her, he could ring the bell and she would come see what he needed. He loved ringing it and she loved responding.

As she laid it beside his hand in the casket, she looked up at me and said that from now on every time she heard a bell ring it would be daddy telling her that he loved her and still needed her. Some people are born knowing things the rest of us spend our entire lives trying to learn. Brittany is wise beyond her years. She adds color to my life and I am so blessed to have her here with me to help me understand the complexities of the world.

So many people came to pay their last respects. I never sat down once. I was glad that I had worn comfortable shoes. Everyone was so shocked and they all wanted to know what happened. I must have repeated the story hundreds of times and my throat was getting sore and I went through boxes of Kleenex.

I had doubted whether or not to have calling hours, but the experience turned out to be very healing hearing everyone say how much they loved and respected Steve and how much better their lives had been for knowing him. People I didn't know told me things about my husband that I never would have known had they not come to say goodbye and told me their stories. With every person's comfort, my pain was eased little by little.

When Steve's father, Dino, passed away many years before, Steve was devastated. He loved his father very much and they had a very unique relationship. As we were in the limousine driving to the cemetery on the day of Dino's funeral, Steve looked out the back window and saw the long line of cars following the hearse and he said "Dad would be pleased. Look at how long that line is."

Steve often joked about his own funeral and would say "All I care about is that my line is longer than Dad's." I made a point of telling everyone at the calling hours to drive separate cars so that Steve's procession would be long.

When we left the church services and headed to the cemetery, I imagined Steve sitting on the top of the hearse looking back at all the cars smiling that wonderful smile of his.

He got his wish. The line was long — very, very long. Everyone came to say goodbye to him and I'm sure he was pleased.

I decided to spend the next five days at home with the kids before sending them back to school and going back to work myself. I felt that we needed some time to be together to come to terms with what had happened. The past few days had been so surreal. There were times when I felt as though I was someone else, watching myself go through this nightmare. I needed some time for us to be together and heal before I could step back into the real world.

The phone rang off the hook and delivery trucks with flowers, plants and fruit baskets showed up. There was so much food. I had to send most of it home with family and friends.

Kym and Joe were there helping out, but they went home at night. I was so exhausted that I couldn't wait to fall into bed each night and I didn't want to have to worry about anyone else besides myself and the kids.

I realized that I had to get on with life, if for no other reason, for Sean and Brittany. I bought groceries, washed clothes, cleaned the house, paid bills and on Monday got dressed and went back to work.

It's odd — I only remember bits and pieces of the next few months. It was like I was there physically, but emotionally I had died right along with Steve. I remember how hard it was watching everyone going about their lives as though nothing had changed. How could they have gotten over Steve's death so quickly? It made me angry to watch people laugh and be happy or talk about things that seemed trivial. When I think back to that time, I am reminded that I need to be more understanding of people when they are experiencing a loss.

I sat down at my desk on that first day back at work and I felt so alone. This desk that I had sat at for so many years felt so foreign to me. I turned on my computer and started to sort through the pile of work on my desk. I talked to my coworkers, who were trying so hard to be careful not to say the wrong thing. People mean well, but no matter what they say it hurts. Then the phone rang and I turned to answer it. As I said the words I had said thousands of times "Good morning - Waterlink," I glanced down at the phone and saw my personal speed dial buttons. The first button said STEVE. Tears streamed down my face and I had to put the person on the line on hold. Only weeks before, I could push that button and Steve would answer. Oh, how I wished I could hear his voice again.

I realized that nothing in my life would ever be the same. All the things that happened every day would never happen again and I wasn't sure that I wanted to go on living in this new life. I hadn't asked for this to happen to me and I wasn't sure that I was strong enough to survive it. The depression had started to set in and it was in control. I couldn't have stopped it even if I wanted to — and I'm not sure that I wanted to. I cried constantly: when I was talking, when I was eating, when I was driving to work and when I was trying to sleep. Nothing mattered anymore. Nothing brought me joy.

❧ Grief ❧

I honestly don't know why my boss kept me on during the months that followed. I was useless. I cried constantly and was easily distracted. When I look back on those months, I am embarrassed by my behavior. I'm sure I was of no help whatsoever to anyone and probably was more of a nuisance than anything.

On the Friday of my first week back at work, I had a meeting with the lawyer who was handling Steve's estate. He had generously offered to do it for free because of his long-time friendship with Steve. He had just as many questions as everyone else did regarding Steve's sudden death and wondered whether I was going to try to find out what might have happened. I said I wasn't sure, but it started me thinking.

I desperately needed answers to my questions. Maybe the one thing that I could focus on was trying to find out what had really happened to Steve and my quest began. I decided to collect medical

53

records from Dr. Keller, the hospital, the pulmonary specialist and anyone else who I thought might be able to help me understand what had happened.

That very afternoon, I went to Dr. Keller's office and requested a copy of Steve's medical file. They were very reluctant to release the file to me. Did I have the necessary legal documents? They were too busy to copy it right then. Could I come back on Monday? Would I mind coming back and talking to Dr. Keller in his office? I'm sure they were eager to get me out of the waiting room where I was in full view of other patients.

Dr. Keller told me of his shock in coming into his office on Monday and finding out from one of his "girls" that Steve had died over the weekend. He said he had called me at my home as soon as he heard, but that he was told that I didn't want to talk to him. He expressed how surprised he was, I believe he might have even used the word "offended," that I wouldn't take the call. I apologized to him and reminded him that I had been in the middle of arranging for my husband's funeral and had other more pressing matters on my mind at the time. I also added that his call certainly was not the only call I hadn't taken.

Indignantly, he suggested that he shared my pain. After all, he had lost a patient who he had treated for many years and who he respected and admired very much. With every word that came out of his mouth, I became more and more incensed. I asked him what happened and his answer was that he didn't really know. It could have been many things. Then he said something very strange, "I can't believe that I had missed it." I thought, "Missed what? The diagnosis? Being there when he died? The funeral? What had he missed?"

What he said next sickened me. He said, "I believe that you never question God's will. You just accept what happens and move on and never look back and question why or point blame at anyone." I can't remember whether I thought or said out loud, "Well, then I guess it's unfortunate for you that I don't share your beliefs, isn't it?" He wasn't trying to comfort me or help me understand what had happened. He wasn't being compassionate or professional. He was simply trying to protect himself.

I spent the next several weeks going over those medical records with a fine-tooth comb. I read and reread things. I bought a medical dictionary and drove my best friend, Monica — a nurse — crazy with question after question about what things meant in an effort to find out what had actually happened during those last hours at the hospital.

I had begged, Kym and Joe to move in with me and help me out with Sean and Brittany. As I look back on it now, I am certain that I caused a great deal of turmoil in their lives. But, at the time, I wasn't thinking rationally about anything. Subconsciously, I had decided that I needed to see if Kym could handle raising Sean and Brittany because I wasn't sure I was going to get through this.

Since Kym was there, I felt comfortable staying after work to indulge in this obsession that had overtaken my life. Some nights I stayed until midnight and would go home so keyed up that I couldn't sleep at all and then I would go back to work and do it all over again.

I was shocked at what I found out!

In 1976, approximately one month before I met Steve, he had been hospitalized for what he had told me was mononucleosis. He was just getting his strength back when I met him. When he was discharged, they told him he had mono and that's what he believed had been wrong with him. The medical records, however, indicated that he actually had hepatitis.

I truly don't think anyone ever told Steve that he was actually diagnosed with hepatitis. If they did, I don't think anyone ever explained to him how serious it could be. It was before the aids epidemic when no one had ever heard of socially-transmitted diseases or safe sex. Obviously, Dr. Keller wasn't concerned because he never bothered to bring it up once during the twelve years that he treated Steve.

There was a ten-year period of time, between 1976 when Steve was hospitalized for hepatitis and 1986 when he was hospitalized with a diagnosis of early onset diabetes, in which almost all the visits could have somehow been connected to his initial hepatitis episode.

In 1978, Steve saw the same doctor who had admitted him to the hospital in 1976 complaining of stomach pain. He was diagnosed with an ulcer.

Sometime in the early winter of 1981, Steve had what we thought was a flu virus and he was terribly sick for several days. He woke me up in the middle of the night and said, "Look at this." His testicles were swollen to nearly three times their normal size. I called my mom and she told me to rush him to the emergency room. They told us that a virus must have dropped on him or maybe he had a strangulated testicle. Just to be safe, they gave him antibiotics and suggested that he stay off his feet and ice himself down for a few days.

Shortly after that, in December of 1981, Steve went to the doctor because he was having terrible back and side pain. He was also extremely tired. He told the doctor about the visit to the emergency room for his testicles. The diagnosis that time was prostatitis, for which he was put on another antibiotic. Blood work was done and acute viral hepatitis was suspected, but the doctor didn't think that the elevated enzymes were from Steve's liver. He thought it was just a muscle enzyme and gave him a muscle relaxant.

In 1984, Steve, once again, went to see the same doctor complaining of chest pain and pressure in his shoulder. Two weeks earlier we had both had the flu and had missed a few days of work. Steve was diagnosed with bacterial bronchitis. The doctor said that the chest and shoulder pain was most likely residual of myalgia. Even as a layperson, looking back now, I can guess that Steve probably had chronic hepatitis and had given it to me and we were both experiencing the side effects it caused.

In May of 1986, when Steve was 36 years old, he again got the flu. In addition to his past symptoms, he was experiencing excessive thirst, frequent urination, blurred vision and leg cramps. At this same time, his doctor had left town for some reason. I vaguely remember Steve telling me something about him going somewhere to learn some new medical technique or something.

It was at this time that Dr. Keller took over the doctor's practice and became Steve's primary physician. He admitted Steve to the hospital and, even though he noted in the admission sheet that Steve's past medical history showed an episode of mononucleosis with hepatitis and an episode of prostatitis, there was no blood work done to check to see if there might be a connection. Of course, neither Steve nor I ever made the connection because we didn't know that he had ever had hepatitis, but Dr. Keller knew. It wasn't very hard for me to find out after he died that chronic hepatitis is often misdiagnosed as diabetes. Surely, a licensed physician would have known that. When a young man with a 10-year history of hepatitis complained of similar symptoms, Dr. Keller should have ruled out chronic hepatitis before making a diagnosis of diabetes.

Dr. Keller did not rule out chronic hepatitis though. Steve was discharged with a diagnosis of new onset diabetes mellitus — apparently type II. From that moment until the day Steve died 12 years later, Dr. Keller stood by his diagnosis. He never did check for chronic hepatitis.

In those twelve years, Steve was never able to control his blood sugar levels regardless of how careful he was about diet and medication. They were always a little high or, when he took his insulin, too low. It seemed strange to me and I always had a nagging suspicion that the diagnosis was wrong. I spent years trying to help him feel better. He tried using vitamin supplements, he exercised, he drank more water and switched to diet soda. I even put him on a special diet for people who suffer from yeast infections. Had we known that it was hepatitis, I'm sure that Steve and I would have been better able to manage his health problems. It was the missing piece in all of our efforts to figure out what was wrong with him.

After three years of my own painstaking research after Steve's death, I found out from the original pathology report that there was a large mass in Steve's liver. Dr. Keller had known about the pathology report. He had known the day I'd gone to his office for Steve's records. He had known while he was telling me how offended he'd been when I didn't take his call. He had known while he told me that he "shared my pain."

One night after all of my research, I was lying in bed and it hit me like a ton of bricks. If Steve actually had developed chronic hepatitis, what were the chances that I had it too?

All those years and Dr. Keller had never once suggested that I get tested or that we should be concerned. Even when I got breast cancer and he knew it, he never even mentioned it. Was he truly that uninvolved in Steve's case or did he just not give a damn?

I lay there, trying to piece together my scattered thoughts. We'd never used any form of birth control and I had never gotten pregnant. Steve had experienced trouble with impotence off and on during the last years of his life. He was always tired and run down. He had pains in his right side and shoulder for as long as I had known him. He had never been able to control his "so-called" diabetes properly with insulin and diet.

The next day I called my oncologist and told him what I had found out about the hepatitis. He told me to come in that afternoon and get some blood work run. Sure enough, the results indicated that there were signs that I had probably had hepatitis more than once during the past 20 years. Luckily, it appeared as though my body had built up a natural immunity to it. To be safe, I was sent to a specialist for more in-depth testing.

It took a few days to get the appointment with the specialist and then 10 more days to get the results back. Being a breast cancer survivor had trained me well in the fine art of waiting anxiously for results. In my depressed state, I worried even more than usual about what I would find out. What if I had chronic hepatitis? What if my liver had been damaged? What if I got liver cancer and died too? Who would take care of Sean and Brittany? How was it passed from one person to another? Was it only through sexual contact or could other fluids like blood or urine carry it? Could Sean and Brittany get hepatitis from Steve or me? Had they ever been vaccinated for hepatitis?

The results came back and, fortunately, everything was fine. I had, indeed, formed a natural immunity to the virus. Despite the fact that I was not a carrier, the specialist suggested that I get the kids tested, just to be on the safe side. I made an appointment as soon as possible with their pediatrician. The tests came out fine: neither of them were ever infected.

Dr. Keller's actions and inaction affected our family in many ways. He affected Sean, Brittany and me. He affected Steve. He affected Steve's family and friends and co-workers. It made me realize just how much one person's life can affect everyone around them.

For years, Steve thought that his illness was uncontrolled diabetes. He was made to feel like a failure because he was tired and sick all the time, because he was unable to manage his diabetes. He thought that he was less of a man than he should have been. He lived with that feeling of defeat and failure for many years.

The misdiagnosis affected the way I treated Steve. I nagged him all the time about being too tired to do things and not helping me more. In my frustration, I even told him to go to another doctor and find out what was wrong with him or just stop complaining about how lousy he felt. I was tired of hearing about it. I said things that I would never have said if Dr. Keller had given us the facts. I said things that I will always regret and I carry a heavy place in my heart to this day for those conversations.

I'm certain that Steve was also affected by the way that he was perceived by himself and others. He was unable to do every day things that others took for granted. He paid someone to mow his grass and wash his cars. Hitting a bucket of golf balls with Sean drained him. Trips to the grocery store or the mall were often cut short because of his fatigue. He couldn't go to amusement parks with the kids because it would lay him up for days afterwards. We didn't even dance much when we went out to parties because he would get overheated and short of breath.

One night right after Steve died, Sean came to my bed and asked if he could sleep with me. He was sad and lonesome and very worried that something was going to happen to me. Both Sean and Brittany worried that I might die. He crawled up next to me and said, "Can I sleep on daddy's pillow?" After we were settled under the covers, he said, "This is where I remember daddy the most. He sure was a good sleeper."

How sad it was to think that Sean remembered his grandfather this way — that we all did. Steve had spent so much time in bed resting. He rested in the evenings, on weekends, every moment that he could in order to have the strength to do things for himself and his family, in order to do something as simple as go to work each day.

My family, his family, our friends, people he worked with all made jokes about how lazy he was. So did I. We all know differently now. He was not lazy. He was the bravest, most courageous man I'll ever know. It took more strength than I'll ever have for him to do what he did each day.

Who knows what he could have accomplished had he been properly diagnosed and treated? Who knows what he would have thought of himself or what we would have thought of him? Who knew where we would be now?

It was 1976 and I worked in the personnel department of the electric company. A girlfriend was dating a guy and she wasn't sure whether or not he was the right one for her. She wanted to go to a "fortune teller" and asked me to go along with her for moral support. I didn't believe in fortune tellers and thought she was being ridiculous, but I went with her anyway.

Before the fortune teller took my girlfriend into the back room, she offered to do mine for half price.

I had been divorced for many years, but I carried my ring with me on my key chain as a reminder to never be stupid enough to get married again. I reached into my purse and pulled out my wedding ring and put it on my left hand.

Before she started the "session," the fortune teller told me that she didn't read palms or tea leaves or use cards. She said that she had this God-given ability to see my "life map." She believed that we were each born with a map and we were destined to follow it. We all had free will and could chose different paths during our journey, but certain things were going to happen in our lives and we could not change the end result. As I listened, I thought she was a con artist.

I have to admit, she got my past right despite the wedding ring I had slipped on in an attempt to deceive her. She told me that I was a divorced woman with a daughter. She knew that my life had been chaotic and that I was about to begin a new season of my life.

She told me that, in the coming year, I would change jobs, buy a new car, move into my own apartment and meet the man I would marry.

She said that I would be engaged and married in the next year. She saw two more children in my life. Our lives together would be long and happy.

She predicted that my husband would die before me. "I see you in another relationship after your husband passes," she told me that day.

I left thinking that I had just wasted five dollars, but I didn't mind because my girlfriend seemed happy. The fortune teller had told her that her boyfriend was, indeed, the right one for her.

The very next night, while shopping at the local mall, I ran into an old friend. We hugged each other and asked all the usual questions. When I asked him where he was working, he said that he had just got a job working for a new engine factory in town. He said it was a great place to work and told me to come down the next day and he would get me an application and see that it got into the hands of the right people. I don't know why I did it — I already had a secure job at the utility company — but I went down and met him for lunch the next day. Maybe, I just wanted to see him again.

Before I knew it, I was invited for an interview and was offered a job with a salary that was unbelievably high. I was able to buy a car to replace my junker. It was only a stripped-down, ugly green Chevy Vega, but it was brand new and it always started when I turned the key.

Kym and I had been living with my parents for many years. I should have been out on my own long before then, but every time I had tried to move out had been a disaster because I couldn't afford it. We had always lived with a roommate and eventually were forced to move back with my parents for one reason or another. At last, I was making enough money to afford a place of our own in a decent neighborhood not too far from my parents.

I was 27 years old and it had taken me a long time and many stupid decisions to get to this point, but I felt that things were finally coming together for me. Money was still tight. I recycled panty hose by cutting off the damaged leg and wearing two panty parts — each with one good leg — in order to get a useable pair. We ate a lot of macaroni and cheese and baloney sandwiches, but we never missed a meal.

I was paid every other Friday which meant that there were 26 paychecks per year. I had budgeted for two paychecks per month and, in those two wonderful months that I got three paychecks, I would pay off bills that had mounted up. Life was good.

I gave very little thought to how my life was proceeding just as the fortune teller had said it would. I was so wrapped up in the joy the changes had brought about that I didn't take the time to think about why it was happening or if it was supposed to happen. I was just glad that it was.

The summer of the same year, July of 1976, my life changed forever. Tim, a guy who worked in the Public Relations Department where I worked, asked a bunch of us if we wanted to come to a party at his apartment. I told him thanks, but no thanks. My partying days were over. In order to go out in the evening, I had to get a babysitter for Kym, which I couldn't afford. Tim asked me if I would clean his apartment for him. He explained that he and his roommate lived there and it could use a good, thorough cleaning by a woman. He offered to pay me so that I would have enough money to pay for a babysitter. I agreed because I needed the money, but I still had no intention of going to the party.

I asked my mom to watch Kym for me and early the next morning I went to clean Tim's apartment.

I was trying to move the coffee table in the living room when a voice from the stairs said, "Here, let me help you with that." Poor Steve, little did he know that he would be helping me from that moment on for the rest of his life. Actually, even beyond that, because he is still with me helping me through each and every day of my life.

I'll never forget the moment I first saw him. I know this probably sounds silly, but it was as though I had known Steve from somewhere. When I saw him standing there, my heart cried out, "Oh, there you are. I've been looking for you everywhere."

He was wearing a blue bathrobe and his skinny, little bony legs were showing out the bottom. It was obvious that he had just gotten out of bed because his hair was messed up and he was putting his glasses on as he made his way down the stairs. He wasn't exactly what I had always considered "my type," but I was instantly attracted to him.

We talked for a little while and I explained to him why I was there cleaning the apartment for Tim. I asked him if he was going to be at the party that night and he said yes. When I finished cleaning, I rushed home and made arrangements for a babysitter. I spent the rest of the afternoon getting ready. I even borrowed an outfit from a friend of mine.

At the party, Steve and I talked a lot and he asked me for my phone number. When I told him I was leaving, he asked if he could walk me home. When we got there, he came in for a little while and then, out of the blue, he asked me if I would mind if he stayed the night. He assured me that he wouldn't try anything. He just wanted to sleep on my couch. He went on to explain that he had just gotten out of the hospital and he needed his rest and he was sure that Tim's party would go on all night.

Any other time, I would have said no and thought the guy was a total jerk — someone just trying to get lucky — but, for some reason, I felt very comfortable with him. I said okay and went upstairs and went to bed. I was usually very leery of guys I had just met, but I didn't give it another thought. I was sure everything would be alright. The next morning, when I got up and came downstairs, he he was already gone. He had left a note in which he said thanks and he would call soon. I thought he had nice hand-writing.

We were both dating other people. However, his girl-friend lived in Columbus and the man I was seeing was married, so we were able to spend a great deal of time with one another.

At first, he would take Kym and me out to supper several times a week. He hated eating alone and enjoyed our company. My youngest brother played high school football and Steve started going to the games with us.

Steve decided that we could save money if we went grocery shopping and cooked our meals at home instead of eating out all the time. We'd go shopping together, he'd pay for the groceries and come back to my place and fix the meals and I would clean up afterwards. It was perfect.

Most evenings he stayed and, after Kym was settled for the night, we would watch television until the 11:00 news came on and then he would go home. We talked and talked, telling each other things that you only tell a best friend. It was completely platonic for the first three months, which was extremely unusual during the early 70s. Not even a kiss. Occasionally, our hands would brush each others or our knees would touch, but neither of us took it any further. My low self-esteem told me that he didn't find me attractive, but I know now that Steve didn't try anything because he was afraid I would reject him. Little did he know. I can't take any of the credit for our waiting so long. I would have followed his lead. However, my wonderful, self-doubting, gentlemanly Steve never tried.

He knew more about me than anyone else I'd ever known and he gave me advise about everything - my job, my finances, my family — but mostly about seeing a married man. He told me I was too good to waste my time on a man who belonged to someone else. Steve never met the man I was seeing, but he said that he must be a fool if he didn't do whatever it took to make it possible to be with me.

I was 28 years old when I met Steve and it was the most wonderful year of my life. Whenever I'm asked to choose a time in my life that I'd want to go back to, I always say that year. It was the year my old life ended and a new one began.

We were together constantly from August until December. One night, right around Halloween, we were lying on the couch together watching television and he kissed me; and, for the first time, when the news was over, he didn't go home. We had moved into uncharted waters and I couldn't even let myself think about what it might mean. I was afraid that if I acknowledged to myself that I had feelings for him, he might be able to tell and then, like all the other men I'd loved, he would leave. I was so happy having him around all the time and I didn't want to lose that feeling. I pretended to be content with things as they were.

Steve invited Kym and me to go with him to his parents house for Thanksgiving and he bought me a full-length leather coat for Christmas. He gave me money to spend on presents so that Kym would have a nice Christmas and he started staying overnight on Thursday when Kym was at my parents' house.

When he told me that he was going to Columbus to spend New Year's Eve with his girlfriend, I pretended that it was okay with me. After all, we'd both known all along that we were still seeing our significant others. Of course, mine would be with his wife on New Year's Eve and I would be alone. I spent the entire night crying and I knew that I could no longer try and fool myself into thinking that I wasn't deeply in love with Steve. Once again, I had fallen in love with someone I couldn't have.

When he got back from Columbus, he called me and asked if he could come over that evening after Kym went to bed. He said there was something important that he wanted to talk to me about. I braced myself and was prepared for the old "you're a wonderful girl, but..." breakup line. Much to my surprise, he came in and sat down on the couch and without hesitation said "Kathy, while I was away this weekend, I realized that I'm in love with you and I want us to spend the rest of our lives together." A little more than a month later, he surprised me with an engagement ring on Valentine's Day and we were married the following October.

When I told him about the fortune teller and how all her predictions were coming true, he just laughed. Steve was much too logical a person to believe that some old woman could read my "map" and know what life held for me. He just wrote it off to a self-fulfilling prophecy. He said that she had planted the seeds in my brain and then I made everything happen. It was just that simple to him.

Of course, by now I was a true believer. I couldn't wait until I got pregnant and had our two children.

We were totally at the opposite ends on this one — Mr. Logical and Mrs. Emotional.

When we first got married, we both talked about wanting to have a baby together; and, although we weren't really trying to get pregnant, we wouldn't have been upset if it had happened. We never used any form of birth control during our entire time together. There was an immense physical attraction between the two of us and it wasn't for lack of trying that I didn't get pregnant during the first five years of our marriage. I never went to a specialist to get officially checked. However, when I talked to my gynecologist about why I wasn't getting pregnant, she said that there was a possibility that Steve might have become sterile from the time that the flu virus had dropped on him. We just sort of accepted the fact that it just wasn't going to happen. Besides, by that time, Kym was into her teenage years and giving us a run for our money and we weren't so sure that we still wanted any more children.

In 1986, after we had been married for almost nine years, Steve was diagnosed with sugar diabetes. I thought it was strange because he was so young. However, there was diabetes in his family and Dr. Keller said that the early onset was probably brought on by stress. Steve's job was stressful and that, combined with Kym's antics, was enough to convince us that maybe a baby wasn't such a good idea after all. The last thing Steve needed right then was the additional stress that a baby would bring. We, pretty much, agreed that having children together probably wasn't in our future. I remember Steve saying, "Well, I guess that proves that your fortune teller was wrong about those two kids."

Then, in July 1990, after years of thinking it would be just the two of us, we were given legal custody of Sean and Brittany. Sean was 22 months old and Brittany was 10 months old. The words the fortune teller had said so many years before came rushing back to us — "I see two more children in your life" and into our lives they came. We loved them and felt truly blessed to have them. For all the sacrifices that we had to make, we were given back ten times that amount of joy and happiness because we had them with us.

For more years than I care to remember, I had gone through periods of unhappiness. We had everything, each other, family, friends, successful careers, money, possessions, all the things I thought I needed to be happy, but there was always this feeling that something was missing from my life. I couldn't explain it. I should have been happy, but the void inside me was like a whirlpool sucking me down into the black depths of darkness and nothing seemed to fill me with the happiness for which I so desperately longed.

Steve wasn't unhappy. In fact, he couldn't understand what I was complaining about. He encouraged me to go back to college and get my degree. He bought me new cars and took me on wonderful vacations, but something was still missing.

It wasn't until after Steve died and I hit the bottom of that whirlpool that I would finally realize what that something was.

I was certain that Sean and Brittany would be the answer to all my problems. Surely, having these two little ones to take care of and love would make me happy. Don't get me wrong, from the moment they came to live with us, my heart was filled to overflowing with love for them, but the void remained.

Now Steve was a different story. He loved Sean and Brittany just like they were his own. Sean was his buddy and Brittany was his princess. He was the kind of grandfather everyone dreads, the one with stacks of pictures and endless stories. You couldn't avoid seeing them or hearing them no matter how hard you tried, but there was a big difference.

Steve was involved when he wanted to be involved. He did the fun stuff willingly and with his whole heart. When we fought about the kids, which wasn't often, it was always because I was overwhelmed and wanted him to help me more with the day-to-day tasks of being a parent, such as doctor appointments, teacher meetings, homework, babysitters, etc. He would always say the same thing, "Hey, you were the one who wanted two kids."

There were many times when I resented him for taking that attitude, but deep in my heart I knew he was right. Even though he wanted them and grew to love them as much as, if not more than, I did, he had certain limits when it came to how involved he would get. It was always a sore spot between the two of us. It had nothing to do with his love for Sean and Brittany or even his love for me, for that matter. It was just how it was.

Maybe, somehow, he knew that eventually I would have to do it all myself and that this would make the transition easier. Because the love, guidance, financial security, morality and spiritual faith he always gave so willingly are all still with us. He gave us what we would need when he was gone.

Only now do I see that sometimes by not giving people what they think they need you actually give them what they will truly need someday to survive.

In 1993, on the Monday after Christmas, at the age of 45, I was diagnosed with breast cancer. I had a spot under my right breast where I kept getting a bruise. I had small breasts so it was fairly easy to check for lumps. I felt something there, but it was very small and I thought it might just be one of my ribs or something.

I went in for my yearly mammogram and my gynecologist recommended that I see a surgeon, who recommended that we remove the lump. He agreed that it was very small and that it was probably nothing to worry about, but he'd rather be safe than sorry.

On January 11, 1994, Kym's 25th birthday, I went into the hospital for my surgery. The surgeon talked to Steve afterwards and told him that he felt fairly certain that it was not cancer. He would know for sure after he got the results of the biopsy back in a few days. I never once even let the thought that I might have cancer cross my mind.

On the day that I went in to get my stitches out and find out the results, I planned on going by myself. Steve, however, felt that he should go along with me just in case. Maybe the surgeon had called him and told him to come with me. I doubt it, though, because I think I would have been able to sense his concern. I truly am more apt to believe that he just intuitively knew that I would need him to be there with me.

My surgeon was very young. I could almost have been his mother. I had teased him before the surgery about whether or not he had ever done this type of thing before. He laughed and assured me that he had and actually with much success. Over the years, we became good friends and I respect him greatly both as a surgeon and as a human being.

I'll never forget the moment he told us I had cancer. He walked into the room with my chart and set it down behind him. He pulled his chair up close to me and touched my knee with his fingers. He started talking about how the results came back positive and that the growth was very small and that we probably caught it in a very early stage. He went on to say that there were several options we could consider about the next step . . . .

I wasn't listening to what he was saying. When he said "positive," I just fell apart. I started crying and if Steve hadn't been there I don't know what I would have done. I said, "Wait a minute. Are you telling me that I have cancer?" He answered, "Yes." Then, in my usual direct manner, I asked him, "Am I going to die?" He told me much later that he was thrown for a moment. No one had ever asked him that exact question so bluntly before. He never hesitated, not even for a second, and said, in a very comforting tone, "I certainly hope not. I'm going to do everything I can to make sure that doesn't happen."

He left us alone for a little while so that we could have some time to come to terms with what we had just heard. I cried and cried and beat my fists against Steve's chest. I remember thinking that they must be wrong. Why would God give me these two children to raise and then give me cancer and have me die and leave them? Steve didn't say a word. He just held me as tightly as he could and we cried together.

When the doctor came back, he discussed my prognosis and told me of my options. He gave me the name of an oncologist that he recommended I speak with regarding the next stage of my treatment. He told us that we should call him the next day he would be glad to set up the appointment with the oncologist for us if we wanted. He stressed the fact that we had to act quickly. The longer we waited, the worse my chances for survival were. He was so kind and understanding, but he made very clear the urgency and gravity of the situation.

Steve took me back to work so that I could get my things and we could tell my boss and coworkers that I wouldn't be back for a while. Everyone was so wonderful and comforting and helpful, but I don't remember anything anyone said. All I could think of was that I had cancer. Me — not someone in the paper or on television — but me.

That night as Steve and I lay in bed, he held me in his arms and I could tell he was just as scared as I was. Steve was a man of few words, especially when he was faced with something of this magnitude. His usual manner was to make a joke out of everything. It was how he coped. There was nothing funny, though, about what was happening to us.

I said to him "Oh, God, Steve, I don't want to die." He assured me that he didn't want me to die either. The words that he said next were what gave me the courage to go on and the confidence to know that everything was going to be alright.

"Kathy, listen to me. You are going to be fine. In the first place, I can't raise these kids by myself and in the second place, there is no way you can possibly die." I asked him how he could be so sure and he said, "Remember the fortune teller. She's been right so far, hasn't she? Well, she said that we would live a long, happy life together and that I would die first and then you would get remarried. Well, I'm still alive and, as long as I'm here, you aren't going anywhere."

He may very well have saved my life at that moment because, throughout the weeks of radiation and the months of chemotherapy, I never for one moment doubted that I would live. He was right — as long as he was still alive, I wasn't going anywhere.

I didn't realize it then, but I can look back now and see the theory of "knowing" at work. I believe, beyond a shadow of a doubt, that I survived because I was so certain that I would.

That was over ten years ago and I am now officially a "breast cancer survivor." Thanks to God and a wonderful surgeon and most of all to a wonderful husband who stuck with me through the whole thing — no hair, no energy, no sex. It didn't matter to Steve. He may not have always known how to say it, but he showed me that he loved me by being there for me when I needed him the most.

Shortly before he died, one of Steve's friends, Lenny, stopped by to visit. He, along with the rest of Steve's immediate family, had gone on vacation with us the previous summer and he had come over to give us a check for his share of the expenses.

I had called him on the phone and left a message on his answering machine, kidding him about hiring someone to come collect the money. He lived about an hour or so away and he showed up at our door one Sunday, unexpectedly, with the check. He came in and visited for a while and we laughed about my phone call. He said that he was sorry the check was so late in coming, but he just hadn't been able to find our address to mail it.

I now know that there are no coincidences in life. My phone call was out of character for me and he had mailed us Christmas cards every year, so I know he had our address somewhere. I believe that his visit was meant to be because it was the last time that he saw Steve before he died.

Steve was in his robe on the couch and he looked pretty sick and I was getting on him about going to see a different doctor. Steve had been sick for so long that I had started to take the attitude that either he make the appointment to see a specialist or I would make it for him. I know I was being controlling, but I'm sure other married couples have that same conversation. You just reach a point where you are sick of making suggestions that aren't heeded and you are so tired of hearing the other person complain that you just get fed up.

That is exactly the point that I had reached. Dr. Keller had been treating Steve for this cough for over five months and his health had never improved. In fact, it seemed like he was getting worse. I had very little faith in Dr. Keller's professional abilities and Steve and I fought about it often. I thought Dr. Keller was egotistical. Steve felt that just because he was a doctor, he knew what he was doing. I, along with many other people who knew Steve, couldn't understand why he had such faith in him.

One of Steve's closest colleagues tried to explain it to me after he'd died. He said that Steve was a very hard-working professional who was extremely knowledgeable about his job. He took his work seriously and made it a point to keep himself informed of any changes or new laws that might affect his work. He was a true professional in every sense of the word and he just assumed that everyone else treated their profession in the same manner. He trusted his doctor because he saw him as a professional. He would never have doubted for a moment that he didn't know what he was doing or that he was being negligent in any way. He trusted him with his health and his life just as others trusted Steve with their money and investments. It would never have occurred to Steve that another professional didn't hold himself up to the same high standards to which he held himself.

During Lenny's visit, we started talking about the fortune teller and, for the most part, we were just making light of the whole thing. Steve told Lenny that, if he died, he wanted everyone to know that this jerk that I was supposed to marry next wasn't going to get a penny of his 401(k). He had worked hard for that money and he'd be darned if my next husband was going to live fat and happy off his retirement money. We laughed. It was all just a joke.

Steve said, "Besides, I'm not going to die. The fortune teller said that we would live a long, happy life together." I remember commenting that 20 years was a pretty long time and he answered me with, "Well, maybe so, but I'm still waiting for the happy part." Again, we all just laughed.

That conversation has come back to haunt me many times.

There are so many things about Steve that were shared by just us. Those are the things that I miss the most.

He loved anything mechanical — computers, televisions, VCR's, stereo equipment. He would have loved DVD's. One of my most vivid memories is of him sitting in front of that stereo making cassette tapes for us to play in the car. After he died, I found one he had made for me where he talked to me in between the songs and told me what the songs meant to him with regard to our relationship. What a priceless treasure.

He played music all the time. When I play his tapes, the kids sing along and know every word to the songs. He taught them to love music and not be afraid of singing out loud or dancing in public. Sometimes when I am feeling low, one of his favorite songs will come on the radio and I know it is him telling me he is still there and that I should cheer up.

He took me on great vacations. He hated to read and never could understand my love of books. He took great pride in his appearance. He loved the Indians and the Browns. He never quite forgave Art Model for selling the Browns.

He had an extraordinary memory. He could tell you anything

about history. He knew all the presidents and vice presidents, all the states and their capitals, all the wars and who won and in what years they were fought.

He was a marvelous cook. He made the best spaghetti sauce. His lasagna was out of this world. On Sunday mornings, he would get up early before the rest of us and start making french toast and would wake us to say it was ready. Sean and Brittany speak of it now, longingly.

He didn't dance very well, but he didn't care. He danced anyway, mostly slow. He would dance fast with me for a while until he got winded. During the last few years, we took to what he called "table dancing." He was too tired to dance, but he would sit next to me at the table and hold me and pretend that we were dancing.

He loved it in the fall when we would change the clocks and move them back an hour. He would be so excited that he got to sleep for that extra hour. He always had trouble getting to sleep at night and he would stay up late watching television. He snored like a freight train and, during the night, it would wake me up. I miss it now.

He had a wonderful laugh. It was honest and spontaneous. When we would go to a movie or watch TV and something was funny, he would laugh out loud. He laughed that same sincere laugh when the kids would do something that he enjoyed. I have a video tape of him giving a speech at work that shows him laughing. I've played it so often that I sometimes worry that it might wear out and break.

Sometimes when we were alone together and we would get quiet for a few minutes, my mind would be racing and I would be thinking about how I should tell him something that was on my mind or ask him a question. He would reach over and touch my hand and say, "What?" as if he knew what I was thinking. It wasn't something that happened only occasionally. He did it often. It was as if he could read my mind. Sometimes he would actually answer the question without my saying anything.

I am still finding out things about him that even I didn't know. Sean and I were in the car waiting for Brittany one day and he said to me "Do you know what Daddy used to say when we were in the car waiting for you? He'd say, "Should we leave without her?" Then we'd all laugh and the two of us would say "Yeah, yeah! Leave without her." Then Sean added, "He was so funny. I sure do miss him." Me too.

If I had to say what I miss the most, it would be his touch — holding my hand, brushing a hair away from my face, straightening my collar, rolling over in bed at night and laying his hand on my arm. When we would walk into a room together or through a crowd or a doorway, he would put his hand on the small of my back and guide me. Such a little thing to miss so much.

I've come to realize that before Steve died I was living life on a day-to-day basis, taking everything forgranted. If I've learned one lesson from this whole experience, it is that there are no ordinary moments. Every memory I have of him, no matter how ordinary, is precious.

Sometime during the first month after Steve's death, I started doubting whether or not I was up to the challenge of raising Sean and Brittany without Steve. I was alone, frightened, confused and depressed. I wasn't sure that I wanted to go on living without Steve. What I really wanted to do was run away from all my responsibilities and quit my job and get an apartment and go to bed and never get back up again.

I asked Kym and her husband, Joe, to move in with us so that I could see how they interacted together. There had been a lot of abuse in their relationship, but they had been together several years and, despite their many problems, it seemed as though they really loved each other. In my need to escape life, I tried to convince myself that it would work out.

She was almost 30 years old. She had a husband to help her. Maybe this was the logical time to let her have them back, but I loved Sean and Brittany so much and I had to make sure that they would be okay first. I didn't want to just shove them out the door and send them to live at Kym's. They had experienced enough change in the past month or so and I wanted to make this transition as easy as possible for them.

Kym and Joe had their own space — a bedroom, bath and family room. We shared the kitchen and laundry room, but they had their privacy. In my confused state, I decided that, if things seemed to be working out, I would move out and let them live there with the kids. That way Sean and Brittany would still be living in the house that they grew up in and would be able to go to the same school and play with their neighborhood friends.

At first, things seemed like they were going to be fine. Kym had been working at a convenience store as a cashier and I told her that I wanted her to quit and stay home with the kids. I gave her $100 a week so that she wouldn't feel that she had to give up the little extras that her paycheck had allowed. The plan was that she would get up and help me with the kids in the morning. I also asked that she help with the housework, do her and Joe's laundry, be there after school when the kids got home, help them with their homework and help start supper.

Joe was working as a roofer and made decent money, but he had a child from another relationship and the state deducted child support payments directly from his paycheck. His driver's license had been revoked and he had large court fines that he was supposed to pay on every month. They had a lot of past-due bills from hospital stays when they had no medical coverage and they wanted to file for bankruptcy. I felt that it was important that they get themselves situated financially so that they could start out on the right foot. I paid all the living expenses and let Joe keep his paycheck.

At my suggestion, they had given up their trailer and had lost a lot of money in the process. To make up for that loss, I bought Joe a brand new Kia so he had reliable transportation to and from work. His job required that he drive to different job sites every day and he needed to know that he could depend on his car for transportation.

He was driving without a license and worried constantly about getting stopped by the police so I gave them the money to pay off his court fines and helped him find out what he had to do to get his driver's license back. I also paid for the insurance on the car. Several thousand dollars and a few weeks later, he was finally legally licensed to drive a brand new, insured automobile.

We went on a family vacation in Florida for a week. Just to give you an example of how insane I was at that period in my life, I rented a 39-foot mobile home and drove it to Florida over Easter break. Steve's mom and his sister and her son went with us. The six of us drove the mobile home down and met Steve's brother and his wife and two children at Universal Studios and then we went down to the Keys for a few days.

I invited Kym and Joe and Joe's son to come with us. The three of them flew down so Joe wouldn't have to miss much work. It was a disaster from the start. Joe had never been on a plane before and he was nervous about flying. Their flight down was delayed for mechanical reasons and they arrived at the hotel almost six hours late. Joe had been drinking to help him stay calm on the flight and they had been fighting all day. They continued to fight on and off for the rest of the trip. I spent part of every day trying to patch things up between them. One or the other of them threatened to catch the next plane home on a daily basis.

Being with them all day and night for a whole week made me realize how volatile their relationship really was. I can see now that it helped me begin to understand that I had to stop looking outside myself to fulfill my needs. It also filled me with even more despair. I couldn't wait to get home. Any thought that I ever had regarding the possibility of Kym and Joe taking responsibility for Sean and Brittany's upbringing flew right out the window. I knew that I had to pull myself together and stop feeling sorry for myself. Sean and Brittany were depending on me and I was all they had left.

I had hoped that the vacation to Florida with Steve's family would be a healing experience for me. Actually, it turned out to be very painful. It was too soon. It had only been a month since Steve's funeral and I still needed to be comforted. If Steve were alive, he would have held me and comforted me, but he was who I was grieving for and I had no one with whom I could share my loss.

I thought I might find that comfort by being with other people who loved Steve as much as I did. I can see now that I was being very self-centered. What I hadn't been able to remember was that I wasn't the only one suffering. They were trying to deal with their own pain. They didn't want to dwell on it or talk about it. They needed to get away and heal, to focus on something other than their loss. My presence made it impossible for Steve's absence to go unnoticed. I sensed their need to distance themselves from me and it made me feel even more alone. I wanted to talk and they wanted to pretend nothing had happened.

I came back from vacation feeling worse than when I left. First, my illusions of Kym and Joe being able to take care of Sean and Brittany had been shattered and then my plans of finding comfort in the presence of Steve's family didn't work out. I had never felt more alone in my entire life. I was able to see that my personal expectations had set me up for disappointment and I had no one to blame but myself.

I kept in touch with Steve's family after we got back, but conversations and visits were infrequent and strained. I was operating on automatic, trying to work every day and attempting to provide a normal daily routine for Sean and Brittany. I was working with the bank and my attorneys trying to understand my financial situation. I was also still obsessed with Steve's medical records. Everything was piling up and I was on the verge of an emotional breakdown.

When I thought nothing else could possibly go wrong, I received a phone call in early June from Steve's sister saying that the family had gotten together in Toledo at Steve's brother's house over the weekend and had discussed what to do about changing the family trust now that Steve was no longer alive.

After Steve's dad died, Steve had set up a family trust for his mom, which divided all her assets equally between her three children and their families upon her death. This was what Steve did for a living and I'm sure that he set it up to protect her estate from taxes and such. When my attorney went through Steve's papers he came across the trust and I decided to give it to Steve's brother. Maybe he would want to have it changed to show that Steve was deceased now rather than having to deal with it should, God forbid, anything happen to his mom.

For reasons I didn't fully understand, Steve's mom, brother and sister and their spouses had decided that they were going to change the trust so that it would now be divided between just their two families. Lynn said she wanted me to know that we had been dropped from the trust entirely. She made a feeble attempt at trying to justify their decision. Thinking, I suppose, that it would make me feel better, she even mentioned that they momentarily had thought about leaving Steve's share to Sean and Brittany, but, in the end, even decided against that option. She was rambling on and on and I was crying so hard that I couldn't breathe. I think I hung up on her in mid-sentence. I was devastated. All I'd heard was that we were no longer considered to be part of the family now that Steve was gone.

As I look back at the whole experience now, I can be more objective and see where they probably felt justified in their reasoning and that there was more than likely no intent on their part to cause me emotional pain. But, at that moment, all my childhood insecurities came rushing back and I was once again a little girl who no one loved. I didn't care about the money, but I needed their love more than ever and they had reaffirmed to me once again that I was not deserving of love, not even by this family I had been a part of for over twenty years.

My thoughts became very delusional. I felt so foolish. Over the years there had been several times when it was casually mentioned that we weren't "blood," but Steve always just laughed it off and said that his mom didn't really mean it the way it sounded. This just proved to me that she had meant exactly what she had said. The more I obsessed about it, the more I blew it out of proportion. How they must have hated having to tolerate us "outsiders" for all those years. Finally they could be rid of us. It was the final blow. I wrote them a horrible letter and mailed it to them telling them how I felt and made a conscious decision to never speak to them again for the rest of my life.

It was just my depression speaking; but, at the time, it all made perfect sense to me.

Two weeks after the trust fiasco, things with Kym and Joe came to a head. Joe started collecting unemployment claiming that he had been laid off because there wasn't any work. This seemed strange to me because he worked as a roofer. It was spring and business should have been booming. He was home all day and he and Kym started fighting all the time. Supper was rarely started, dishes were piled up in the sink, homework wasn't being done. The minute I got home from work the two of them rushed out the door and were gone all evening.

Even though I was paying all the bills, buying all the food and giving Kym $100 a week, they still asked me for my credit card or money so they could get gas for the car or buy clothes or rent videos or get cigarettes.

I had known since our vacation together that things were not going to work out and that I would have to eventually tell them that I felt they weren't prepared to raise the kids. I had decided to offer to get them a little house of their own and help get them settled. I was just waiting for the right moment to talk to them about it, but things kept getting worse. Neither of them were working, they were fighting all the time, both verbally and physically. Joe was becoming frustrated having to follow my rules and I suspected that they were smoking marijuana.

I took Sean and Brittany to school on my way to work in the morning because Joe and Kym were never awake that early. They got home from school at about 3:30 in the afternoon and I didn't get home until 5:30, so they were only there alone with Joe and Kym for two hours every afternoon. Brittany didn't seem to mind so much, but Sean asked me if he could start going to after-school daycare again. He had never liked going to daycare and I thought it was strange that he had asked to go back. It was so obvious that he didn't like being at the house with Joe when I wasn't there. All the signs were there, but I completely missed them. I still find it hard to believe that I could have been so blind. I let Sean down by not picking up on his cues to me.

While we were on summer vacation a few years ago, Sean told me that Joe had punished him by beating him with a belt. If he cried when he was punished, Joe would whip him again. Joe told him that he had to learn to take his punishment like a man and stop being such a baby. I asked him why he never told me about it while it was happening. He told me that Joe said he would get a worse beating if they ever found out he had told me. Of course, I didn't know any of this back then. I wish I had, but I didn't.

I was so angry as I listened to him tell me this painful memory, not just at Joe but at myself for not seeing what was going on all those months. I can only imagine the helplessness and feelings of despair he must have felt thinking that he would never be able to escape from this terrible life.

All too soon, it was June and school was out for the summer and Sean once again told me he didn't want to spend the whole day at the house while I was at work. I knew that I had to do something so I decided to send Sean and Brittany to a day camp at a local swim club. Brittany didn't want to go to the camp for the whole day, so I compromised and said I would pay for a family membership to the pool so that they could go to camp half a day and then Kym could come and spend the afternoon there with them until I got home from work.

That night Kym told me that she had decided that she didn't want to go to some snooty swim club every day and that she wanted me to install a swimming pool in the back yard. They went out the next day while I was at work and looked at aboveground pools, but Joe said they were too flimsy. Without discussing it with me, they talked to someone about installing an in-ground pool in the back yard. Kym said that the guy could come the next day to give us an estimate. Things were spiraling way out of control and I, of course, said no way. It was too expensive and it wasn't what we had originally talked about.

Kym blew up and there was a big fight about my never keeping my promises. She accused me of forcing them to lose their home and ruining their lives. They said I had lead them to believe that they would be living in the house and raising the kids alone. They wanted me to start looking for an apartment as soon as possible so that they could get on with their lives. Joe said he was tired of me telling him what to do all the time. He was the man of the house now and he felt Sean and Brittany would never see them as their parents as long as I was still there.

I told them that I was sorry that I had misled them. I tried to explain to them that I had been very confused when I'd asked them to live with us, but I had come to my senses. I realized I was wrong and couldn't go through with it. Since it was my fault that they had lost their trailer, I even offered to give them enough money to get a little house of their own. I had paid off all of their bills, bought Joe a brand new car and was willing to give Kym my brand new Suzuki Sport. They were in much better shape than they were prior to coming to live with us. I felt I was being more than fair.

We argued for what seemed like hours. There was no reasoning with them. They would have kept it up all night if I'd let them, but it was late and I was too tired to fight any longer. I told them I was going to bed and that we would talk about it again the next day when everyone had calmed down. As much as I hated to admit it, I was very scared and I went to bed not knowing what to do next.

The next night was a major turning point for me. It changed my fear to anger and motivated me to make important changes in my life.

Through his job, Steve had been involved with the local chapter of The Boy Scouts of America over the years. Because of this, they had arranged for a dinner to honor Steve and had asked me to bring the kids to accept a gift in his memory. We had been planning for this night for a long time and, when I came home from work that night, Kym informed me that Brittany couldn't go to the dinner because she had been disrespectful to Joe. I told her I was taking her anyway and braced myself for yet another confrontation.

I went upstairs to talk to Brittany alone and I told her to get dressed. I didn't care what Joe said. She was going to that dinner. My eight year-old granddaughter told me, "It's okay, grandma. Just take Sean and go without me. I knew when I smarted off to Joe that he'd punish me, but I didn't care. It was worth it to tell him off. Don't worry, I'll be fine." Against my better judgment, I agreed to go without her.

Sean put on his new double-breasted suit, just like Steve's, and we went off to the dinner. It was such a wonderful evening for Sean. They spoke about how Steve had been such a help to them over the years and how much he would be missed. Then they asked Sean to come forward and accept a plaque in Steve's honor. They also gave him a pin for his lapel and some flowers for Brittany, who unfortunately couldn't be there. He was so proud. It was the happiest I had seen him in a long time.

When we got home, he rushed in to tell Brittany all about what had happened. "Brittany, look what they gave us for daddy." Kym jumped up and shouted at Sean, "He wasn't your daddy. Joe is your dad now. I don't want to hear another word about your grandpa ever again. He is dead and you better get used to it." She turned to me, still shouting, "We want you to move into the downstairs bedroom tomorrow. See how you like living like hired help. You can stay down there until you find another place to live. We don't want another house. We want this one like you promised."

Brittany became very upset and started crying and yelling, "He was too our dad. This is our house. You can't tell us what to do." Kym picked up a large glass of ice water that she had been drinking and threw it right in Brittany's face.

"That's it. I've had enough. Get out right now," I shouted at them.

"We aren't going anywhere and neither are Sean and Brittany. They're my kids and I can do whatever I damn please with them. I'd rather see them dead than let you take them away from me again." She pushed me and I fell backwards onto the couch.

The kids rushed to my side crying and clinging to my legs. I was shaking and I knew things were getting out of control. I took Sean and Brittany upstairs to my room and locked the door. Kym and Joe raged on downstairs for what seemed like hours. The kids finally calmed down when I assured them that I would never let anyone harm them and that everything was going to be alright. They fell asleep in my arms with their clothes on, one on each side of me. I lay awake all night and tried to figure out what to do. I knew that I had to get us out of there safely, but I wasn't quite sure how I was going to do it.

Both Sean and Brittany were being tutored three days a week over the summer break and the next day was tutor day. In the morning, I woke Brittany up and got her dressed. She had the first hour of tutoring and I always took her over on my way to work. I usually went to work and Joe took Sean over to the tutor's house when Brittany was done. I still didn't know what I was going to do. I would just take it one step at a time.

I didn't want to raise any suspicions, so I decided not to wake Sean up and take him with us. There were no noises coming from downstairs and I figured that they would sleep in late because they had been up so late fighting. I took Brittany over to the tutor's house, which was only five minutes away.

Panic set in, as I realized I'd made a mistake by leaving Sean at the house alone, and I rushed back and found him still asleep in his bed right where I had left him. I woke him up and had just started dressing him when Joe came up to the kitchen and yelled, "What are you doing back home?"

"I took the day off work so I can go look for an apartment and I thought I'd come back and take Sean over to the tutor so you could sleep in for a change."

He wasn't falling for any of it and ran downstairs to wake Kym up. By the time she woke up and got upstairs, Sean and I were already out the door and in the car. I got Brittany from the tutor's house and took off as fast as I could.

The rest of the day was hectic. I called my brother, Bob, and his wife, Pat, and told them what had happened and asked them if we could stay with them until I figured out what to do. Like so many times before, when I had asked a favor of them, they didn't hesitate for a moment.

Bob stayed with the kids while I went to see the attorney who had worked with us when Kym had given us custody of Sean and Brittany more than eight years before so I didn't have to go into a lengthy explanation of the entire situation. He seemed a bit confused because I had just the month before told him that I was thinking about giving the kids back to Kym.

He suggested that I take Sean and Brittany somewhere safe, somewhere that Kym and Joe wouldn't expect us to go and that I go to the police department and have them escort me to my home to get some clothes and whatever else we needed to survive for a few weeks. While I was doing that, he would start eviction proceedings to get them out of my house. He said that I would have to have them evicted because I had invited them to live there. I couldn't believe what I was hearing. I had to leave my own home and take the kids somewhere else until I could legally have them evicted from my home.

He also suggested that I go to all the utility companies and have everything shut off as soon as possible. It was his experience, in cases like this, that people usually left a lot sooner when there was no water, cable, air conditioning, lights, etc. In the next few days, I would find out what good advise this would turn out to be.

Later that night the police escorted me, my sister and her sons to my house with my SUV, her station wagon and the boys two trucks to get our belongings. Kym and Joe moved out two days later. My attorney had been right about the utilities. I turned off everything: the phone, the cable, the electricity, the gas and the water. The house was in shambles, but that wasn't important to me because we were safe and they were out.

I went over the next day and had the locks changed, but I didn't feel comfortable going back there to live yet. I was afraid that they would come back and try to take the kids. I wasn't taking any chances.

Fear is a great motivator. My entire outlook on life had changed and things would never be the same again.

I didn't really have a clue about where we would live as we left the house. We could stay with my brother for a while, but I knew it would be an imposition.

I considered taking the kids to my mom's house. She had moved to a retirement home and left her house almost completely furnished. I knew, though, that it was the first place Kym and Joe would look for us. So, we just unloaded all of our belongings at mom's and went to Bob's house.

I was running out of options when my boss offered to let us stay at his house while he was with his family on vacation. They would be gone for a month and the timing was perfect.

I was very appreciative and extremely nervous both at the same time. Their house was beautiful, filled with antiques and Sean and

Brittany were two fairly active children. However, it was a perfect hideaway and it gave me a whole month to figure out what I was going to do. If nothing else, I would just move back home at the end of the month. It turned out to be yet another blessing for the three of us because we were all pretty shaken and needed to feel safe and secure.

I enrolled Sean and Brittany in a two-week day camp for young kids who had recently lost a loved one. It's mission was to give children an opportunity to talk about their feelings with other kids who were going through the same thing. They talked and wrote and drew pictures about what they were feeling and it gave them an outlet that wasn't limited to the adults in their lives. I was a little apprehensive at first, but the outcome was tremendously successful. If nothing else, it helped them to realize that they weren't the only ones who were going through this painfully, live-changing ordeal. There were kids who had lost a sibling, mom, dad, grandparent or pet. Everyone had lost someone and they all were confused and needed help sorting out their emotions and understanding what they were feeling.

On the last day, they wrote messages to their loved ones and released helium-filled balloons in honor of the person that they had lost. I thought it would be emotional, but most of the kids were laughing and seemed to view it as a happy ending to their two weeks.

Sean and I walked out to the field and he let go of his balloon and watched as it grew smaller and smaller. "Goodbye balloon," he said, "Go to Heaven and find my grandpa." Then he ran off to play with some of his new friends.

I found Brittany sitting by herself on a hill holding her little red balloon. When I asked her if she was okay, she looked up at me with angry eyes and said, "No! I'm not going to let mine go. You can't make me."

She hadn't spoken to me much about Steve's death in the three or four months since the funeral. If Sean and I talked and cried about Steve, she told us that we needed to get over it and stop being so sad. She reminded us on a regular basis that he was in Heaven with God and that he was fine and wouldn't want us to be sad. She always viewed it so matter-of-factly that I never worried too much about whether or not she was handling it well.

But, when I put my arms around this beautiful little girl and rocked her in an effort to comfort her, she started crying uncontrollably. I didn't even try to talk to her. I knew that she needed me to just hold her and let her cry all those tears that she had been holding in for so long.

After about 15 minutes, she wiped her face on my shirt and said, "Grandma, do I have to let this balloon go?"

I said, "Of course not. If you want to keep it, you can."

She looked up at me and said, "I want to let it go so that it will make grandpa happy, but I'm afraid that when it's gone he will be gone forever too."

We sat for a long time and said nothing. When Sean came over to see if we were ready to go, we walked towards the parking lot. One of Brittany's little hands was holding mine and in the other she clutched that balloon as tightly as she possibly could. Just before we got to the car, she stopped and let it go and said, "Goodbye, grandpa. I miss you. Don't forget me."

I hugged her and gave her a kiss on the cheek and told her how proud Steve must be of her for being so brave. The balloon seemed to follow our car for a few blocks and then it drifted away.

As soon as I decided that things were going to change, everything just seemed to fall into place. All I had to do was open my
mind to new possibilities and the necessary opportunities presented
themselves to me.

The three of us moved back home the first part of July and it
didn't take long for me to decide that I was going to sell the house.
It really wasn't as impulsive as it may have seemed to some people.
The summer before he died Steve and I had actually started looking
for lots so that we could build a new house. We even had the floor
plans picked out. It was something we had thought through care-
fully and decided to do. It was one of the few things from our life
together that hadn't changed. Besides, there were a lot of painful
memories associated with Kym and Joe in that house now for all
three of us. I wasn't sure where we would move, but I knew I was
going to do it.

I hadn't felt safe sending Sean and Brittany back to the tutor and
I knew that they would be even further behind when school started
again in the fall. There were only two more months until school
started and I had to start thinking about what I should do about
schooling for them.

They both have dyslexia and school had been a struggle for them.
The decision to have them attend a Catholic grade school was one
we never regretted. It was invaluable in providing them with a strong
religious base and a sense of community. However, because they attended a private school, we had difficulty getting them the amount of
special tutoring they needed. Just the year before, we had moved them
to our local neighborhood public grade school because they were set
up to work with children who required assistance. It was better, but
there were so many kids in their class that it was almost impossible
for the teacher to give each child any individual attention.

Steve and I had started looking for a private school that would be better equipped to help them. When Steve first considered changing jobs, we had sent letters to several schools in various parts of the country thinking that, once we found a school, he could find a job nearby. Instead, he had taken a job locally that he really loved and we decided not to follow up on any of the out-of-town schools.

I had just started thinking of where we might move and checking out local school districts when I received a letter from one of the schools we had applied to the previous spring. It was in Cincinnati, which was a four-hour drive from where we lived. It sounded great, but I wasn't sure I had the strength to move so far away and start a whole new life for the three of us. I stuck the letter in my purse and forgot about it, until a few days later, when I was talking to a business associate on the telephone who happened to live in a town near Cincinnati.

He asked how I was doing and I mentioned that I was looking for a school for Sean and Brittany. I told him about the letter and was surprised when he said he knew someone connected with the school. He had only good things to say about it and encouraged me to check it out. However, he also said that there was a waiting list and it was often difficult to get admitted, but that he would make some calls and see what he could find out.

I really had no intention of moving out of town until that phone call. A few days later, I was in the car driving the kids to their admission interviews. We filled out the necessary paper work, had some required testing done and talked to several people who said they would call us the next week and give us their decision.

Growth

Sean and Brittany were accepted, but the administrators wanted us to come back down to take some additional tests to help determine what department would be best suited to their individual needs. Once again, we went and spent the weekend there.

Before leaving, I was looking for a book to take with me to read while the kids swam in the pool. I opened a box of books my mom had given me and grabbed the one on the top of the pile. It was a book that my brother, Scott, had given to my mother when my dad had died. It appeared as if it had never been opened.

I didn't even read the little write up on the back of the book to see what it was about. I was in a hurry and just grabbed it or it grabbed me. I'm not sure. It was a small paperback entitled "Embraced By The Light" by Betty Eadie. I had no idea, at that moment, what a difference this book was about to make in my life.

It was a short book with fairly large print and it was an easy read.

It was about a woman who, at the age of thirty-one, died and came back to life after undergoing surgery for a partial hysterectomy. Her journey revealed to her a wonderful secret about the meaning of life. It helped her understand why she was here, how all that she had experienced in her life had been for her good and that sometimes it had taken extremely painful experiences to help her grow spiritually.

The message I received from this book was life changing. I learned that I had to let go of the past, change my heart, forgive myself and move forward. The author explained that we had all been sent to Earth to learn from our experiences and that it was okay to make mistakes. In fact, it was actually part of the process. There was no need to punish myself or be concerned about others' judgment of me. She said that God had always loved me and that the void I had felt for most of my life was the result of my forgetting that He loved me. The pain I was experiencing would be the motivation I needed to help me remember and end the unexplained sadness that this separation had caused me for so long.

For many months, I had been engulfed by the incredible fear that I couldn't handle everything myself, tormented by enormous guilt for not doing enough to save Steve and submerged in the depths of sorrow over my sudden loss. I was terribly depressed and I didn't know whether or not I wanted to go on living.

Several people had tried to help me find comfort by turning to religion. Father Dyer, friends and people I knew through work. After Steve's funeral, my cousin, Karen, had written me a beautiful note saying that she was praying for me and she enclosed a little booklet about God. She said that our Grandma had brought her to the Lord and that she was truly grateful to her for that.

I don't know why this book worked where other attempts had failed. Maybe the timing just hadn't been right. Maybe it was because the book didn't talk about religion as an institution, but instead it spoke of spirituality and finding the light that burns inside of each of us. Maybe I had to get past the shock and pain and anger before I could be open to hearing that God loved me. I know for certain that picking that book out of that box was no accident. It was placed in my hands by angels and it taught me to replace fear with love and to be grateful for the challenges that had been presented to me. I learned that my healing had to come from within and that I would be given all that I needed if only I would let God know that I was prepared to receive His guidance.

It was just the first step in a long journey, but, for that moment, just believing that life really didn't end with death and that I would someday be together again with Steve gave me the strength to make the decision to rejoin the human race again. I had a long road ahead of me, but I was on the right path.

I was having some difficulty figuring out where I stood on the subject of God and religion. Over the next few days, I started a mental review to see what I had always thought about the subject as opposed to what I had just discovered.

While I was growing up, my parents had always taken us to church on Sunday morning and I guess you could say that I believed in God. I always thought of God as someone who knew everything you did all the time and that bad behavior would keep you out of Heaven. I also thought that the bad things you did when you were closer to the time to die, you could say you were sorry and you'd be forgiven and get to go to Heaven instead of going to Hell. Hell was where people went when they didn't have time to repent before they died.

When I was older and the decision to attend church became mine, I decided that you didn't have to attend church to be a good Christian. If God was truly everywhere and saw everything, then I didn't have to be at church to contact him. And contact him I did — when I didn't start my period, when I was speeding and saw a cop ahead at the side of the road, when my child was sick, when I was applying for a new job or needed a raise. You know, all the times that really counted.

The rest of the time I did pretty much whatever I pleased. I figured that I wasn't going to die for a very long time and that I could always ask for forgiveness some day. Until then, I did whatever made me feel better for the moment. I used all kinds of excuses for my behavior — I was broke, I was lonely, I was unloved, I was a single mother. I convinced myself that I deserved to have some fun every once in a while because I had such an unusually hard life. I don't ever remember praying for anyone else or even saying "thank you" when my prayers were answered.

When I met Steve, my feelings about religion changed a little bit. He was raised in the Catholic church and had always attended Catholic school. He told me so many wonderfully funny stories about his life in the Catholic school system. I always thought that comedians exaggerated when they told jokes about nuns, but Steve assured me that it was true. He had behaved out of fear. Not fear of some "maybe God" that would punish him someday if he didn't go to confession, but fear of a real, flesh and blood woman in a black and white habit who could break all his fingers if he acted up.

During all the years that I knew Steve, he never once went to church on Sunday morning or to confession. The only times I had known him to attend church involved a wedding, baptism or a funeral. Yet, for some reason, he decided that he wanted us to get married in the Catholic church. Since I had already been married and divorced, I had to go in front of the Diocese in Youngstown to get my first marriage annulled. This was not an easy thing to accomplish, but it really seemed important to him, so I did it.

After we had been married for many years, he told me that it was more for his parents than for himself. He also thought that his church was beautiful and would be a wonderful place to be married.

Even though he complained and said he hated attending Catholic school, somewhere along the line I think it made him a better person. He was honest, loyal, moral, decent, trustworthy, compassionate and forgiving. You don't just come by those attributes by accident. It may have had something to do with the way he was raised or by the friends he hung around with at school. Who knows? Something made him the way he was, but I give a lot of the credit to those nuns. Fear or no fear, they gave him his foundation.

When we got custody of Sean and Brittany, he said that it was important that we take them to church or send them to Catholic school because it would give them a solid base on which to build their own moral convictions. I'm sure it helped, but their real teacher was Steve himself. He set a good example.

When Steve died, I "believed" in God. I was pretty sure he existed. During my deepest moments of pain and depression over losing Steve, Father Dyer and the congregation at St. Joan of Arc Church were of great comfort to me, but I realized that maybe I didn't have as much time to ask for forgiveness as I had thought. I started thinking about changing some old habits.

I missed Steve terribly and felt that I hadn't gotten a chance to say goodbye to him. I was thrilled when I read that there really was a Heaven and that Steve was, indeed, up there watching over us and could even hear me when I spoke to him.

"Embraced By The Light" described a Heaven that was beyond my wildest dreams. It was written in such a way that you couldn't help but believe this woman. It gave me new hope that I would see Steve again some day.

I actually began my journey for very selfish, ego-based reasons. I needed to know that Steve could hear me and that I could say some things that had been left unsaid. I needed to ask his forgiveness and this book said he would hear me.

It also reconfirmed to me that the fortune teller was right. There really was a "plan" that was determined before I was conceived which I had brought to Earth with me. We weren't just down here wandering around aimlessly. We each have a life purpose or a "destiny" to fulfill while we are here and it helped me to begin to understand why Steve had died and, even more so, why he had lived.

I was so uplifted by this book that I read it three times that weekend. Every time I read it I learned something I had missed the time before. I couldn't believe that I had never heard any of this in all those years of Sunday school. Why hadn't someone told me this before? It would have made my life so much easier if only I had known this all along.

The answer to that question would be a long time coming. I had a lot more growing to do before I would be ready to completely understand the answer. I know now that the reason no one ever told me any of this before was because I didn't ask the question. Only after the pain was unbearable and I needed to know what to do to start healing my wounds, did I look up and ask God, "Why didn't You tell me all this years ago? Why did You let me suffer the agony of not knowing how to fill the void I carried with me for so long?" Loudly and clearly the reply came back, "Why did you wait so long to ask Me?"

I returned home from that trip with no doubt in my mind that I was supposed to make this move. On the following Monday, I turned in my notice at work, told my family and friends that I was moving and went about making all the necessary arrangements.

People told me I was making a big mistake. They said that losing a spouse was a major, life-changing circumstance and that all the books say that you shouldn't make any rash decisions immediately following this kind of loss. There were a few who encouraged me, but the majority of my family members and friends were very concerned that I had, indeed, lost my mind and was headed for trouble.

My entire life I had been afraid of lots of things — heights, the dark, being alone in the house, things that lived under the bed, confined spaces. I was even afraid of sleeping with my back to the bedroom door for fear that someone would come in and grab me.

One night early in our marriage, Steve was having trouble sleeping and he asked me to switch sides of the bed. I said absolutely not. I couldn't sleep on the other side. He just accepted me at my word and put his pillow at the other end of the bed and slept upside down and never asked me why. Then several years later, on the first night in our new house, we went to bed and I got in on the opposite side of the bed. Steve went nuts. He said, "I thought you couldn't sleep on that side of the bed." When I told him that I had to be on the side farthest away from the door he cracked up. I don't know why I thought that if I wasn't close to the door, it would be any better, but I insisted on sleeping with someone else between me and that door.

From the moment I read Betty Eadie's book, I have never once been afraid of anything — well, maybe the Flight of Fear at Kings Island. All traces of fear were gone. Knowing that I am not alone has made me feel safe. God's love has replaced the fear. As terrible as losing Steve had been, it has taught me to be strong. He had always been my strength and now he would still be here with me, perhaps in ways that were impossible before. All I had to do was ask for help and, sure enough, in came the cavalry — Steve, my dad, his dad, my guardian angels and most of all, God. I would never again feel afraid. I now knew that I was not alone, had never been alone and would never ever be alone again.

My last day at work was July 31st and Sean and Brittany's first day of school was August 27th, which meant I only had three weeks to get ready to move.

One day while I was packing, a friend of mine, Sue, from up the street stopped by to see how I was doing. She was surprised to hear I was leaving town and expressed concern over my quick decision to do so. We talked for a while and then she asked me if I would mind if her husband, Jonathan, would come down to see me. She said that something had happened that had changed his life and she thought I might want to hear about it.

Our kids were about the same age and had played together in the neighborhood for several years. Steve and Jonathan were what I would describe as casual friends, talking to each other in the front yard occasionally and making small talk when they dropped off or picked up the kids. You know things that men talk about like cars, sports, work and the weather. When Steve bought his new car,

Jonathan bought our old one from us and cleaned it up and sold it and that was a topic of discussion for a while. Men communicate differently than woman do.

Two summers prior to Steve's death, we had invited Sue and Jonathan and their three boys to spend a few days with us at the house we always rented in Nags Head in The Outer Banks. They had family close by and were going to visit them during the same time period that we were going to be down there so it worked out perfectly. During those few days, Steve and Jonathan formed a new found bond. They sat on the pier in the evening and shared a few beers and talked about how hard it was to raise kids and how great it would be if they didn't have to go back to work. After that vacation, when we would see Jonathan in the neighborhood, Steve would always comment on what a nice guy he was or mention how much he had enjoyed the time they had spent together at the ocean.

The next day, when Jonathan and I talked, he said that what he was about to tell me was rather unusual. He went on to say that he had wanted to talk to me ever since Steve's funeral, but that the time never seemed to be right. He also explained that he was afraid it might upset me.

His words came out slowly, "On the morning that Steve died, I had worked the afternoon shift and had come home and went right to bed. While I was sleeping, I had a very upsetting dream. I dreamt that I was in a room that appeared to be in a hospital and that there were several doctors and nurses working frantically around a patient's bed. From the way they were hurrying and from what they were saying, I felt as though the patient might be dying. Then, after they had all walked away from the bed, I walked closer in an attempt to get a look at the patient's face. To my surprise, it was Steve."

He went on, "I woke up from the dream in a very anxious state and went looking for Sue to tell her about it, hoping she could help me shake the feeling of anxiety I was experiencing, but the house was empty. Then I remembered that she had mentioned some errands she needed to run and figured they had left without waking me."

"Kathy, that dream was so real that it scared me. I almost called your house to see if Steve was alright. Later, just before lunch, I thought about walking past your house to see if anyone was home, but then changed my mind. I hadn't talked to Steve for a month or so and felt silly and thought maybe I was just overreacting. But I just couldn't shake the feeling that something was terribly wrong. When Sue came home, I never got a moment alone with her to mention it."

"When your sister called Sue later that afternoon to tell her that Steve had died, she immediately came and told me what had happened. I could feel the blood rushing from my face and I had to sit down before I could tell her about my dream."

"I am sure that I was at the hospital when Steve died. For some reason I can't explain, I witnessed what was happening. Maybe Steve hoped that I would call you to see if he was okay so that you would find out he was dying and that he needed you."

Maybe Jonathan witnessed Steve's death so that something would be awakened in him. Maybe he was shown this vision so that I would have proof that these things really did happen. I guess we'll never know for sure, but I do feel certain that he was contacted from the other side and I do know that it has made a profound difference in both our lives.

Somehow, I managed to pack our belongings and put them on a moving truck and move into a three-bedroom apartment about 20 miles from the kids new school.

I had contacted a neighbor who was a realtor and asked her to list our house. My brother, Bob, acted as our go-between. She would tell me what needed to be done and I would call Bob and he would see that it was taken care of for me. Carpet, paint, wall paper, plumbing repairs, you name it and he did it. Sometimes he hired someone to do the work and sometimes he did it himself.

I had always felt a special bond with this wonderful brother, who was two years older than me. I know that without his help, I would have never been able to get our house ready for sale during those six months. Steve was never what you would call a handyman, but the house was badly in need of repairs because he had been so sick the last year of his life. They were all things we could live with on a day-to-day basis, but they would have to be fixed if I wanted to get a decent price for our home. I came back a few times over Thanksgiving and Christmas to check things out, but it was Bob who did all the work.

I had very little hesitation about leaving this town that I had called home my entire life. Kym had finally made me so angry that I could walk away from her without regret and Steve's family had hurt me so much that I didn't care if I ever saw any of them again. The only other thing that might hold me back was my mother.

I had promised my father when he was dying that I would take care of her after he was gone. She was in relatively good health for someone 75 years old. She was overweight, in the beginning stages of diabetes and had undergone surgery to have both of her knees replaced, but, for the most part, she was perfectly capable of taking care of herself. Almost any other elderly person in her condition would have been thrilled to be in such good shape and would have been out enjoying life to its fullest, but not mom. She just laid around her apartment in a very upscale nursing home in her nightgown and watched television. She only dressed when she absolutely had to and she refused to do anything for herself. Someone else cooked her meals, cleaned her apartment, did her laundry, bought her groceries, picked up her prescriptions and paid her bills.

Dad had always done everything for her and I can remember her telling me how angry she was at him for dying before her and leaving her here to take care of herself. She drove all of us crazy with her demands for attention. It wasn't that we had to do things for her so much. That's just part of being a son or a daughter. It was more the fact that she expected it to be done the moment she called. She would call and whine about how she was out of milk or needed a prescription picked up, but she wouldn't ask you if you would mind doing it. She always waited until you would offer and then when you would say, "I'm going that direction later this afternoon," she'd say that she had to have it right that minute. The worst part was that she rarely gave any of us the slightest hint that she appreciated anything we did for her.

Despite all that and the fact that we never really got along during my entire life, I doubt that I would have been able to muster up the courage to break my promise to my dad and leave her behind if it hadn't been for the way she acted when Steve died. If ever there was a time that I thought she might be able to stop focusing on herself long enough to be a real mother to me, I thought for sure it would be at this my time of greatest suffering, but she proved me wrong by being even worse than usual.

She was upset because no one came and got her in the middle of the night when Steve was dying. When she found out what had happened, she said, "Why did everyone else get to be there and not me?" It was as if she had missed out on some party or something. She called my brothers and sister and complained that she was being neglected the days between Steve's death and his funeral because everyone was so busy with me. The final blow was at the calling hours the morning of Steve's funeral. I was up by the casket while the priest was saying the Hail Marys and I could hear my mom's voice in the background saying, "How many times are they going to say that? Why are we in here? I thought they did this stuff yesterday. These seats are awfully hard." Finally, my sister threatened to take her outside and she shut up for a few minutes. When she came over to see me outside afterwards, I thought for sure she would put her arms around me and comfort me. Instead, she said, "Oh, Kathy, this has been so hard on me, I don't know if I'll even be able to go to the cemetery." As always, this was all about how it affected her with no regard to what it was doing to me.

The last of my problems was solved for me, once again, by the very person who I was concerned about leaving behind. She made my decision to move away easier. I felt bad for my brothers and sister because of the additional burden it would place on them, but I had other things to worry about. She would complain whether I stayed or left so I left with a clear conscious.

I forced myself to get our new apartment organized enough for us to live in it, but there were boxes in corners that I never unpacked the whole six months that we lived there. While the kids were at school every day, I went back to bed and slept or stuffed my face with junk food while I watched hour after hour of mindless television shows. I was terribly depressed, but I truly didn't realize it then. I thought I was doing fairly well. I kept telling myself that it had taken a lot of guts to do what I had done and I was very proud of myself. After all, I was paying the bills on time, there was always food in the house, our clothes were clean and I had even managed to get through the holidays in one piece.

Truth be told, I wasn't okay. I was alone in a new city hundreds of miles away from my home. I didn't know anyone and I had never felt so alone in my entire life. I knew I had to find a way out of this hole into which I was digging myself deeper and deeper. I had all the signs of major depression. I couldn't sleep, didn't care what I looked like, cried constantly and had shut myself off from all outside contact. I thought about calling someone and getting an antidepressant, but I didn't know who to call and couldn't organize my thoughts enough to follow through on it. I got some St. John's Wort from a health food store and took it for a while, but it didn't seem to make much difference in how I felt.

Then, just like everything else that had happened since Steve died, another "angel" came into my life to keep me moving on my path toward enlightenment. I had the television on all the time. It didn't matter what was on, I just needed the distraction. I started watching Oprah every day when she was just starting her "Remembering Your Spirit" shows. She had such wonderful guests with uplifting stories about how they had found a new meaning in their lives by remembering their inner spirit. A lot of what they were saying reminded me of "Embraced By The Light" and she talked about journaling and how important it was in helping to understand and heal pain. It sounded like it was right up my alley.

I started my journal. Instead of writing it in longhand in a diary, I did it on the computer. It was very healing and it helped me start dealing with the pain, anger and guilt I was feeling over Steve's death. I needed to talk about how I was feeling and most of my friends and family were very uncomfortable talking to me about it.

More than anything else, I wanted to talk about Steve. It was very healing for me to talk about what had happened, but I seldom got the opportunity. Instead, I poured my heart out in my journal. On some days I wrote for hours without even being aware of how much time had passed. Sometimes, the pain it brought to the surface would rip at my heart and I would become physically ill. Many times a depression would set in that was so deep that I didn't bathe for days at a time. I would get up and take the kids to school in my pajamas and then get right back in bed when I got back and stay there until the school bus dropped them off at 4:00 in the afternoon. Other days, I just got in the bathtub and stayed there for hours.

At some point in my journaling, I realized that I was never going to find the peace I was looking for until I took a long hard look at myself to figure out what it was that caused me to feel so unworthy of being loved. A grief counselor I had spoken to suggested that low self-esteem could almost always be traced back to some specific childhood experience. She felt that, if I could figure it out and come to terms with it, maybe I could finally let it go and put it to rest once and for all.

It took a long time to sort through all the garbage and come up with the answer. At different times during that period, I wanted to quit and just forget about it because it seemed like it was just adding to my pain. I was so angry at my mom for the way she had acted when Steve died that I just wanted to keep being angry at her. It was an emotion that I had always felt when I thought of her and it was hard to imagine what it would be like if it was no longer there.

My mother and I had never gotten along from as far back as I can remember. I can truthfully say that I cannot remember one time when I was growing up that she picked me up and held me in her arms and told me that she loved me, not even when I had skinned my knee or fallen off my bike. I do, however, remember her yelling at me. When I was real little, I can remember trying to avoid her. I figured that if she didn't see much of me, then maybe she wouldn't catch me doing something wrong and that she would think I was a "good little girl." But, even if she only saw me once a day, she would yell at me about something and act like she wished I weren't there.

Very early on, I realized that my older brothers hardly ever got yelled at for anything and it seemed like they got into a lot more trouble than I did. So, I even tried dressing like a boy for a while hoping that it would make things better. If it was possible, it seemed to make things even worse because my mom started yelling at me for being such a tomboy and started dressing me up in frilly, fancy dresses, which I hated. To this day, I still feel uncomfortable when I am wearing something too feminine.

Someone once told me that, when you are an adult and you are placed in a situation that makes you feel uncomfortable and your reaction is somewhat childish, it is because something of great significance happened to you as a child that was so painful that a part of you just stopped maturing past that point. So, when something happens to trigger that emotion in you, you revert back to the age you were when that pain began.

I often revert back to the age I was when my mother started rejecting me. I'm sure that she actually had begun withholding her love from me and treating me differently at an even earlier age, but the age I realized it was eight. That was when my father, who I adored, also started rejecting me in order to appease my mom. When I am

112

in a situation where I feel unloved, I almost always begin behaving like a confused eight-year old.

To better clarify how my relationship with my mother affected who I became as an adult, I am going to tell you a story about my baby brother, Craig. Hopefully, it will help you understand how my perception of not being loved by my parents caused me to become the type of person who was obsessed with making sure that no one else would ever have to go without the love I felt I had been denied. My relationship with Craig was the basis for my role as a caretaker/enabler and the list of people whom I would impose this role upon grew longer and longer as the years went by.

I was a pre-teen when Craig was born and his birth was an important turning point in my life. It was the first time in a very long while that I actually got a positive response back from someone that I loved. Babies have a way of loving you unconditionally.

My mom had to have a hysterectomy shortly after Craig was born. I'm not sure why, but I believe that it was necessary due to complications from the pregnancy. I vaguely remember that my Aunt Alberta kept Craig at her house for a while when he was first born to help my mom out until she regained her strength. Being a child, I had no understanding of the physical or emotional strain that having a hysterectomy puts on a woman. Later, when I was in my mid-thirties, my dad told me how close mom had come to dying after the surgery. He told me how scared he was that he might lose her. It must have been a terrible time for her. I realize now that she was only 34 years-old and she'd already had five kids at home to take care of and now there was another baby who would demand her attention 24 hours a day. The hysterectomy threw her into early menopause, but I was too young to comprehend any of that at the time. All I could see was that she was rejecting Craig just as she had always rejected me and I wasn't going to let that happen to him. I became his champion.

Shortly after they brought him home from Aunt Alberta's house, mom and dad decided to use the old "let him cry until he falls asleep" approach to getting him to go to sleep at night. On the second night, I lay awake in my bedroom, which was directly above mom and dad's room, listening to Craig crying for what seemed like hours. First, mom had given him to Aunt Alberta and now she couldn't even get her fat, lazy butt out of bed to hold him when he was crying.

I was only 12 years old and, up until that night, I had never been what you would have called a willful or disrespectful child. I marched downstairs into my parents' bedroom and announced to them that if they didn't want to be bothered with Craig, I would be more than happy to take him up to my room and care for him properly.

My father thanked me for the offer, turned me around on my heels and sent me back upstairs, informing me that they were perfectly capable of caring for Craig themselves, thank you very much.

I was furious. I lay in bed that night and made a promise to Craig that I would do everything in my power to make sure that he was loved by someone. If my mother wasn't going to love him then, by God, I was. Looking back on it now, I can see how immature I was acting and realize that I didn't see the entire picture; but, at that moment, I only saw life through the eyes of a very young girl who had felt unloved for many years. When I looked at that darling little baby, all I could see was a helpless child who needed to be loved, and I became his "protector."

Taking care of Craig was never a burden to me. I was at the age where I was too young to baby sit and too old to play with dolls anymore, so having Craig to take care of was wonderful. I bathed him, fed him, changed his diapers, took him for walks and rocked him for hours in this old wooden rocker in my mom's room. I remember vividly the song I would sing to him as I rocked him. I sang it to all the babies who came in to my life from then on — Kym, Sean, Brittany. It was "Always." Maybe you've heard it. It goes like this:

I'll be loving you, always
With a love that's true, always
When the things you plan
Need a helping hand
I will understand, always, always

Days may not be fair, always
That's when I'll be there, always
Not for just an hour
Not for just a day
Not for just a year
But always

He was the first of many "babies" brought into my life and I loved him with all my heart. I have never been able to resist picking up a newborn baby and snuggling my nose down into the crook of its neck. Once a bunch of my friends and I were discussing what we would do if we didn't have to work and could just volunteer our time somewhere. The first thing that came to mind for me was working in the nursery at a hospital during the night shift rocking newborns and letting them know how special they were before they went off with their new parents.

That was many years ago and much has changed in each of our lives. Craig had his problems with mom and dad just like the rest of us, but he chose to solve his problems differently. He left and

115

shut that part of his life away. Unfortunately, he left more than just his parents behind. He has distanced himself from his siblings, too. Over the years, he has made occasional appearances at weddings and graduations and funerals, but it is very obvious that he has made a conscious decision to stay away. That's okay. He has the right to live his life as he chooses, but I miss him and am grateful for the role he played in my life. He was the first victim I ever rescued and he set the stage for many to follow. I hope that someday maybe he'll read this and know that his big sister still thinks of him often and will be loving him "always."

Not long after that, just about the time I was going through puberty, my mom started working nights as a nurse's aide at one of the local hospitals. It was very physical work and she often came home exhausted. In my constant quest to win her approval, I bent over backwards to help her. I helped with chores and watched my little brothers. I tried to be very cooperative, but that didn't work either. Lots of my friends were close to their mothers and talked to them about everything, but not me. My mom never taught me anything about makeup or dating or falling in love. I learned about reproduction from a movie we saw with our Brownie troop. She never talked to me about anything personal at all. Finally, when I went to high school, I just said the hell with it and did things on purpose to drive her crazy. If she was going to hate my guts and ignore me or yell at me all the time, I might as well get the satisfaction of actually deserving it.

I never understood what I had done to make her dislike me so much until once when I was in my early twenties. For some reason, I had stopped by my parents house in the middle of the afternoon, which was something that I never did. I think I had a doctor's appointment close by and didn't have to go back to work and was just killing time until it was time to pick Kym up from the babysitter's house. We started talking and she told me a story about when I was born.

She said that when she told my dad she was pregnant again for the third time in less than five years, he told her that he already had his two sons and that she could go ahead and have her "girl" now. She said that at first she was very excited when the doctor told her in the delivery room that I actually was a girl.

She said, "Well, from the moment your dad laid eyes on you, you were his little angel. He loved you so much. The older you got, the cuter you got and the more he paid attention to you and told everyone how beautiful you were."

"I never quite forgave you for taking him away from me."

I couldn't believe what I had just heard. She was jealous of her own daughter. She saw me as competition and because of that she could never quite love me the way a child should be loved by her own mother. It didn't make me feel any better, but at least I finally understood what I had done wrong to make her hate me so much.

Her jealousy caused my relationship with my father to be unnatural too because he soon realized that she would get mad when he paid attention to me and everything changed. From then on, he never again told me I looked pretty or that I was his little sweetheart or interacted with me the way most fathers and daughters do. Quite the opposite, he actually went out of his way to avoid me as much as possible. The only time he was nice to me was behind my mother's back. He never took my side in any argument, even if he knew I was right. He'd come up to my room after one of mom's tirades and say, "Please, honey, I know it's hard, but please don't upset your mother. Please, just do this for me."

117

The stage was set for all my future relationships. I had always been a good student and this lesson was an easy one. If you love someone, in order for you to keep them in your life, you must accept the fact that there is someone else in their life that is more important to them than you. If you want to continue being part of their life, you must keep their secret in order to keep that other person from finding out about you. You must also work twice at hard at pleasing this man that you love and, above all, you must never complain about the circumstances of your relationship, no matter how limited or one-sided it may be, or it will be over for good.

When I was in high school and my dad and I were both working downtown, he called me and asked me to go to lunch with him. He told me to meet him at his office. He was the international sales manager in a marketing department of a large company and he worked in a very nice office not too far from where I worked. He introduced me to all the other people who worked with him and then we went to a fancy restaurant for lunch. It was so wonderful and I was so happy. We talked more that day than I could ever remember talking before. He asked me about my life and acted as though he was interested and told me how proud he was of my getting a co-op job working half-days while I was still in school. I walked him back to his office and, just as we got to his door, he turned to me, obviously unaware of the bubble that I was floating in three feet off the ground. This man who I loved so much and needed so desperately to love me back said, as if it were the most normal thing in the world, "Oh, by the way, please don't tell your mother that we did this. She would be furious."

The bubble burst and floated high into the sky never to be seen again.

Once I realized the reason that I felt so totally unworthy of being loved, I needed to figure out how it had affected my life and my relationships. This whole process wasn't getting any easier or less painful, but it was the middle of the winter and I didn't have anything else to do so I trudged on ahead.

I had always been a bit of a cynic when it came to love. All my life, all I ever wanted was for someone to love me. I wasn't very pretty or popular and I had very low self-esteem. I never really expected anyone to truly love me because I had been taught that I wasn't deserving.

So, I was really surprised when, very early in my freshman year in high school, I met a guy a year older than me who played on the football team with my older brother and we started dating. I don't know what any of the other girls thought, but in my eyes he was the best looking guy in the school. At first, he seemed to really like me and we spent all our free time together and I think most people considered us a couple. For a little while, I actually thought that maybe I had been wrong about myself and had found someone who I loved that actually loved me back.

He was my first boyfriend and I loved him with all my heart. All I wanted to do was make him happy. In the beginning, he wrote me these wonderful notes. They weren't sentences, but just thoughts he would have about me. I had never felt so happy in my entire life and I would have done anything for him. Like a lot of other teenagers, there was a lot of sexual attraction between us and it wasn't long before we "went all the way." This was in the early '60's, back when most girls didn't have sex with their boyfriend, but I loved him and didn't want to take the chance of losing him. It seemed like this was something he really wanted and I loved him so much and would have done anything for him. How could I deny him something he needed me so desperately to give him? I truly thought that this would be what would keep us together. I wanted to ask my girlfriends if they were "doing it" but we didn't talk about those things back then.

Most of my friends had boyfriends that they went steady with all through high school and I thought we would be together forever just like everyone else. I became overly possessive because I was so desperate for love. If he didn't call me every night, I worried. I did everything I could think of to arrange ways we could be together. We were young and immature and I'm sure that I was smothering him. He didn't have a car and he didn't really like to go to school dances or movies so we spent a lot of our time riding around in the back seat of his buddy's car making out. He loved my dad but couldn't stand my mom so he never wanted to come over to my house.

Things went steadily down hill and, for the next few years, I chased him and he ran from me. Finally, when he was a senior, one of his buddies from another school fixed him up with a friend of his girlfriend to go to their senior prom. We still saw each other off and on for a little while after that. Eventually, though, she became his girlfriend and I was someone he called when he wanted to have sex. He went away to the service and I heard that they were engaged. He married her on my birthday and it broke my heart. He was my first true love and the person I had chosen to give my virginity to and, for reasons I couldn't understand, he had decided that I wasn't the type of person he wanted to marry. I don't think I ever truly recovered from that experience. He reconfirmed to me that I was not worthy of anything but a secretive, secondary, totally one-sided relationship.

After that, I decided that there were only two ways to get boys to pay attention to me: by being funny or by having sex with them. I also found out that they laughed with me and fooled around with me, but they never considered me a "girlfriend" or took me out on a date in public. It hurt terribly, but being a funny slut was better than being alone. I wasn't very pretty and I never really fit in with everyone else. I had to work hard at staying on the fringes of any crowd I ran around with. I always knew that no boy would ever choose me to be his girlfriend and, as odd as it may seem, it was okay with me. I had been conditioned well. I was just happy to have something that vaguely resembled a relationship. For the few short moments I spent having sex, I felt loved and I needed so desperately to be loved that I chose to not think about how much worse I would feel after it was over.

Even my relationship with Kym's father was based on this same scenario. He was really good looking and a real smooth talker. I was so thrilled when he showed an interest in me. We dated on and off for over a year right after I graduated from high school. Everyone in the crowd we ran around with knew that we were seeing each other. As time went by, he started giving me lame excuses about having to work late or something and he would actually be taking some other girl out on a date. Sometimes he would even ask me if he could use my brand new Camaro because his car wasn't running. When he would bring it back, I would drive him home and we would have sex and then I would go home.

After a while, I knew what he was doing and so did all our friends, but, as usual, I just accepted it. Then I got pregnant and my parents forced him to marry me and it wasn't fun for him any more so he split. He actually got another girl pregnant while we were married. We got married in June and separated in November. Kym was born in January. We got divorced in March and he married his girlfriend two days later. Their baby was born in August and he left us and never looked back.

I was never the type of girl who guys would see out somewhere and were compelled to ask to dance or talk to for a while in order to get my phone number. There were times when I went out with my friends and sat at the table alone all night while they danced and had a good time. There was that one thing that I could do better than most girls though.

It was the early '70's and a lot of girls were having casual sex, but because I needed to be loved so much and because the only time I felt loved was when I was having sex with someone, I did everything I could to make the experience so wonderful for my partner that he would want to come back and do it again. My only connection to love was sex and I perfected it the way other people perfected their artistic talents. It was how I valued myself. I fantasized about someday becoming good enough that someone might want to stay forever.

By the time I met Steve, I was so hardened that I never for one moment during the entire time we were together truly believed that he really loved me. There was an intense physical attraction between the two of us, but I was certain that, once the initial thrill wore off, he'd leave just like all the other men in my life. He was seeing someone else when I met him and I knew it. The number two position was very familiar to me.

When we got engaged I was so happy. We had begun planning an October wedding and I was beginning to think this might actually be the real thing. When he came over the day before Easter and told me that he couldn't go through with the wedding, I could tell that he felt bad. He tried to explain that it wasn't me. He said he loved me, but he was afraid of taking on the responsibility of raising Kym. Through my tears, I told him it was okay and that I never really expected him to marry me.

A few nights later he came over and apologized. We made up,

but the memory of that experience stayed with me for the rest of our life together. When he told people the story about us getting back together, he always joked about how he only went back with me because I cried. Even after we had been married many years, I woke some mornings and lay beside him watching him sleep wondering to myself how much longer I had before he would leave.

Being married to me wasn't easy. I loved Kym very much and overindulged her. I had created a very spoiled, difficult child and there weren't too many men who would have stuck around through all the problems we went through because of it. Besides, I was no beauty queen. He could have done so much better for himself. Surely, he would figure it out sooner or later and leave me for someone else.

Of course, it never happened. Oddly enough, for a long time after he died, I actually found a certain amount of comfort in knowing that because he had died, at least, it meant that he hadn't consciously made a decision to leave me. I thought I was lucky that he died before he figured out that I didn't deserve him. Being a widow surely must be less painful than being a rejected wife.

Even now, years later, I dream sometimes that he isn't really dead after all. He just pretended to die to get away from me and is somewhere living with some other woman. I run into him in a restaurant or some other public place accidentally and I'm so shocked to see him. He never explains why he did it and I never ask.

During the first few years of our marriage, Steve and I talked a lot about our childhoods and how we felt about our relationships with our parents. He was the third of four children. His oldest brother,

Dean, was a beautiful, blonde-haired boy who died when he was only four or five. I believe the doctors thought his appendix burst, but it turned out to be a blocked bowel or something of that nature. He was the love of Steve's parents lives and his mother never really recovered from the loss. Steve said that he felt that she withheld outward displays of affection to her other three children because she didn't want to love them too much. The time he felt loved by his mother the most was at mealtime. Food was her way of showing people that she cared and perhaps that was the most she was willing to risk.

Then came Dennis, Steve's older brother, who Steve described as very good looking and popular. He was athletic, smart, funny and hung around with the jocks. All the girls loved him and his parents paid for him to go to the local Catholic high school where all his buddies were going. In my eyes, Steve was much better-looking than Dennis, but Steve never felt that way. He loved Dennis very much and he was never jealous of him, but he said that it was obvious early on that love came easy to Dennis.

Steve described himself to me as being a nerd who hung around with the popular crowd. A new Catholic high school opened his freshman year and he worked after school sweeping and emptying wastebaskets to pay for his own tuition. He never had a steady girl, but he occasionally asked someone to a dance or some other social function. He was a good student and tried hard to do well in school and be successful in his career so that his dad would be proud of him. It would turn out to be how he valued himself for his entire life. He worked very hard to be viewed as an intelligent, honest, successful businessman. Just like me, Steve felt that he didn't just deserve love, but that he had to work hard to get it.

His sister, Lynn, was the only girl and the baby of the family. His mother loved her very much and kept her so sheltered for much of her early childhood that she suffered from separation anxiety when she had to eventually leave her mother to go to school. Even though her father had never quite understood what to do with a girl and would sometimes punish her when she was little for something she had done wrong, Steve still felt that his parents' love for Lynn was very obvious and unconditional. No matter how irresponsibly she acted, they were always there for Lynn.

Although I didn't know it when I first met him, over the years I learned that Steve came into our marriage with his own emotional baggage. He had a certain fear of rejection and was never willing or maybe even able to commit himself completely to a close, intimate relationship with anyone. He told me how surprised he was that I loved him so completely and that no one had ever loved him the way that I did. Even though I was able to soften him up a bit, he had a great deal of difficulty expressing his feelings, not just to me, but to everyone. I needed him to send me flowers and cards or surprise me with little romantic moments, but he didn't. In his mind, he showed me that he loved me by providing so well for me and sticking with me through all the turmoil. He was always so practical.

Whenever the subject of flowers came up, he said, "You spend all that money on flowers and then they die and you have nothing to show for it. Wouldn't you rather go out to eat or get a new outfit for yourself?" He could never see that getting unexpected flowers was the most romantic thing he could have ever done and that it would have meant the world to me.

Once when we were in a store he said to me, "Here read this card and then pretend that I sent it to you." If he did, on occasion, buy me a card on Valentine's Day or my birthday, it was always one of those funny ones.

125

The only way he could share his emotions was by being funny and making me laugh. That way, if he got rejected, he could pretend he didn't really mean it. He never just came out and told me that he loved me. He would say something like, "Have I told you lately that I love you?" When I would say yes that I thought he had, he would say, "Was I sober?" and laugh. He thought I knew he loved me and that I didn't need to hear it, but I did. I was so needy that one hundred times a day wouldn't have been too much.

When I found out that I had breast cancer, although he was wonderful, I so desperately wanted to have him hold me in his arms and say, "Oh God, Kathy, I love you so much. I couldn't go on if anything happened to you." But, what he actually said was, "You can't die. I can't raise Sean and Brittany by myself." I know it was just his way, but I wish he could have been more emotional and less practical every once in awhile.

The only time I ever saw him love anyone unconditionally was when Sean and Brittany were born. I think he felt safe with them. He never held back his love for them in any way because he knew without a doubt that they loved him back. Kids have such a healthy, honest way of expressing their love without reservation.

After Steve died, I talked to Father Dyer about the affect that losing him might have on Sean and Brittany. I thought maybe it would have been easier on them if they had been younger and hadn't known him so well. Father Dyer said that actually they would probably be better off the way things were because they would never wonder for a moment whether or not Steve would have loved them if he had lived. No biological father could have ever loved his children more than Steve loved them. They knew they were loved because he showed them with his actions and told them with his words every single day. I am sure that Steve learned as much about love and expressing his emotions from them as they learned from him.

There is a lot more to being in a committed relationship than just coming home to each other every night. In the dictionary the definition for the word commitment says "to pledge to be responsible for another's care." During the early stages of being in love, it is very easy to be totally involved in the needs of the other person. You are willing to do whatever it takes to make the other person happy; but, as the years go by and things get more and more complicated, you find yourself forgetting your commitment. Eventually you become less and less involved in doing things that will make your partner's life better or happier.

I wish I had loved Steve enough to tell him about my fears. The last few years we were overwhelmed by his illness, my illness, the responsibility of raising Sean an Brittany and our never-ending struggle over Kym. As much as he loved Sean and Brittany, he was never able to get over his anger at Kym for not taking responsibility for her life. There was one rule by which he stood firm: he absolutely forbid me to give Kym money. She was my daughter and I loved her and she had a way of pulling at my heartstrings. Time and time again, I gave her money behind his back. If he found out, he'd confront me. It hurt him that I lied to him, but I was so torn between wanting to help her and not wanting to make him angry. For days after our fights, he wouldn't talk about it and eventually it would seem like it was over, but, of course, it wasn't. It pushed us further and further apart until, finally, we were just two people living together under the same roof. We didn't argue or treat each other badly, but we had forgotten all about love and commitment and sharing our feelings. We forgot to "be responsible for each others care." We were just trying to survive and it was unbelievably lonesome sometimes.

There's a Jimmy Buffet song that goes "I just want to live happily ever after, every now and then." Steve used to play it a lot and I think back now and see that life was not very happy for either of us during those last few years. There were moments, but, for the most part, we were no longer connected in the same way. We had let things get too far out of control and it would have taken more energy than either of us possessed to make things right again. I don't know if he ever thought about leaving, but I can tell you for certain that, if he did, the kids were why he stayed.

We were both dealing with our own inner struggles when it came to love. I couldn't see it then, but I know we both really did love each other. It was just a shame that I never trusted him enough to believe that he would stay and he never trusted me enough to let down his guard and show me his true feelings. I wish we could have let our love for each other exceed our need to be safe.

For most of my life I had felt that I could find the answers to all my questions in books. I had been doing a lot of reading about grief and all the different stages people go through during times of loss. It had been almost a year since Steve's death and I felt that I wasn't making any progress. Some of the books said the magical time was one year, some said two and some said it was different for each person.

I tried to convince myself that my slow progress was because I had not only lost my husband, but my daughter, my in-laws, my job, my home and my entire support system as well. All the roles I had always used to form my identity were gone — wife, mother, in-law, secretary. I was struggling to understand what was left of the old me and trying to figure out who I was becoming. I was so confused. I felt like a lost soul at sea barely keeping my head above water.

As I wrote in my journal day after day, I came to the realization that I was avoiding the real problem and I needed to start being honest with myself about what was really tearing me apart. If I didn't, I would never find any relief from the pain that was crippling me. Sure, I had suffered a terrible, untimely loss and everyone kept assuring me that it was normal for the healing to take time, but there was something else that was holding me back.

There was a secret that I had kept for a long time and I had to confront it in order to start moving forward. This was by far the most difficult thing I had ever attempted. I had a few girlfriends with whom I felt very close, but I had never really felt safe enough to allow myself to be completely honest with anyone. I had spent much of my life trying to get people to like me and because of that I had to pretend to be someone that I was not for a long time.

By all outward appearances, my life with Steve had been wonderful. I had a handsome, intelligent, sexy, funny, supportive, responsible, understanding husband who loved me and provided me with all the comforts of life. We lived in a very nice house in a safe middle-class neighborhood. We owned three cars, went on vacation every year, had many good friends and large families who lived close to us. My job was relatively easy and the pay was exceptionally high for my field. If I wanted something, all I had to do was go out and buy it. Steve never complained about how much money I spent. He invested a great deal of money every month through his 401(k) plan at work and would proudly show me at the end of each quarter how it was growing. Every once in a while, he would sit down and show me how much money we blew every month and try and put me on a budget. But, for the most part, he never really cared about how much I spent. There were only two rules: credit cards were to be paid off every month and no money was to be given to Kym.

He loved to tease me about money. Since he worked in a bank, it was easier for him to take money out of the ATM's than it was for me. All he had to do was go down to the lobby and take money out. So whenever I ran out of cash, I would go to him and hit him up for a few bucks instead of stopping at the bank. His answer was always the same, "What did you do with the five bucks I gave you last week?" Always with the jokes!

I loved Steve and I never once wished I hadn't married him. My low self-worth wouldn't allow me to accept him as he was and not need more from him than he was able to give. I had done something I was ashamed of and the fear that he would leave kept me from telling him the truth.

"Please, Steve, don't die. Open your eyes and look at me. I should have stayed with you last night. Why did I leave? Can you hear me? There's something I have to talk to you about. It's important."

My husband was slowly slipping away and there were only moments left before he would be gone forever. They said he could hear me, but I needed him to be able to talk to me.

"I'm sorry. Forgive me. You know I love you and never meant to hurt you. Please, honey, stay with me. I'll make it up to you. I promise. Just don't leave me."

His blood pressure was dropping so fast and the nurse looked at me with eyes that said it was over. I thought I had all the time in the world, but it was too late for confessions. He was gone.

I had been unfaithful to Steve with the same married man that

I was seeing when Steve and I met. Jim had been part of my life for a very long time and it was not just some casual fling. I had known him for many years before I met Steve. My feelings for him were genuine. I loved him very much. We were very close and we talked on the phone a lot during the years that followed my marriage to Steve. He'd call me to brag about his kids or tell me about a vacation they took or ask me my opinion about a change in his career. Steve knew we talked and never seemed to mind when I told him we were meeting for lunch. After all, his best friend, Linda, was a woman so he didn't think it was strange that I had a close friend that was a man.

Jim was better than having a close girlfriend when I needed a shoulder to cry on about some injustice in my life because he didn't always take my side about everything the way girlfriends do. He gave me his opinion from a man's point of view and told me when I was being unreasonable. I always felt better after I'd talked to him. He said things that I needed to hear, like how nice I looked or how much he missed me and how he often wondered what our lives would have been like if we'd gotten married. For the most part it was just a friendship, but it was a dangerous one. For someone as needy as me, it was far too easy to fall back into this man's arms in a moment of weakness. We should have known that we couldn't just be friends after all we'd shared together in the past.

Being with Jim was easy because he already knew everything about me and I could just be myself. I didn't have to worry that he would find out what a phony I was some day. We were both married now so he was more relaxed because he didn't have to worry that I might want him to leave his wife. In fact, it was just the opposite. I actually encouraged him to stay with her. If he would have asked me to leave Steve, my answer would have been "no." I loved Steve and couldn't live without him. Once we talked about what I would do if Steve ever found out and I told him that I would deny it and that my concern would be entirely for protecting Steve from being hurt.

How could I have thought that what we had done hadn't affected our relationships with our spouses? Every time we were together I was taking something that should have belonged only to Steve and giving it to someone else. If I wanted to be with this man so much, I should have been willing to leave Steve and make whatever sacrifices were necessary to be with him, but I didn't want Jim to be my husband. I wanted exactly what I had. I loved Steve so much and I worried that he might find out and leave me, but I kept on seeing Jim anyway. In my sick mind, I was certain Steve would leave me someday and, by having an affair, perhaps I reconfirmed to myself that he would be justified in doing so.

It seems strange to me now that I carried this burden with me for so long thinking that it was easier to pretend it had never happened rather than admit it and face the consequences. There were so many times when I wanted to tell Steve what I had done, but I just couldn't bring myself to do it. What if he left? What would I do? I always thought I'd tell him someday when the time was right.

Now Steve was gone and I was suddenly confronted head on with the consequences of my actions. The guilt was unlike anything I had ever experienced in my life. Someday was no longer a possibility.

I had been unfaithful to a man who I loved more than life itself, who I had married and with whom I had shared sacred vows. I remember looking Steve in the eyes and saying, "I, Kathy, take you, Steve, to be my lawfully wedded husband. Forsaking all others. To have and to hold, for better or for worse, in sickness and in health, from this day forward — **"til death do us part."** I had meant every word I said. What had happened that allowed me to so casually break those vows? Why was it that I could so easily forget about the part that said "forsaking all others?" I couldn't answer that, but I knew that what I had done was wrong. I just didn't know what to do about it. Steve was dead. I needed to ask forgiveness, but from whom and what made me think I deserved it?

Late one night, the summer after Steve died, just before the kids and I moved to Cincinnati, I was lying in my bed trying to fall asleep. I started thinking about that day over 20 years before when Steve had just come home from visiting his girlfriend in Columbus on New Year's Eve and told me he had broken up with her because he was in love with me. Then I remembered something I hadn't thought about in a long time — how I had met with the married man I'd been seeing the next day to break things off.

I called Jim and asked him if we could meet to talk. I told him that I had met someone and had fallen in love and, to my surprise, this "someone" said he loved me too. I said that we had promised each other that we wouldn't see anyone else and that I was sorry, but I couldn't see him any longer. He was wonderful about it. He said he understood and that, even though he didn't know Steve, he could tell that he made me happy. He thought I deserved a better life. A life he couldn't give me. There was an air of sadness not unlike the feeling you have when you graduate from high school. We knew it was inevitable and the best thing for both of us. It was time for me to move on to a better life, but we were also losing something that had been a large part of our lives for a very long time and we were going to miss each other. It was bittersweet.

I drove back home that night wondering if maybe I wasn't making a mistake. Not because I didn't love Steve enough to give up this man, but because I felt like this whole thing with Steve was too good to be true. For just a moment, I thought that it might have been better to just keep things the way they had been for so long. As strange as it seemed to consider staying with a married man who would never leave his wife, I felt certain that I was giving up a "sure thing" for someone who would more than likely be gone in a few months. No matter how unfulfilling this relationship was, at least it was always there.

When Steve did come and tell me he couldn't go through with the wedding just a few months later, I cried all night and thought about the mistake I had made saying goodbye to Jim. I remember thinking I should have trusted my instincts and not followed my heart. I knew I didn't deserve to be loved the way other woman did. What could I have been thinking?

My mind was racing with all those memories and no matter what I did I still couldn't fall asleep so I tried to distract myself by watching television, but my mind kept going back to Jim. I was all alone and I needed to feel like someone loved me. Not long after that, I called him. I needed someone to comfort me and hold me and make me feel safe. I was very vulnerable and I knew in my heart that it wasn't the right thing to do, but, as always, my need to be loved far outweighed those few moments of rational thinking.

Maybe this was why I had kept in touch with him over the years and why I had started seeing him again after I swore I wouldn't. Maybe subconsciously I knew that someday I would be alone again and that I wouldn't be able to find someone else to love me. He had always loved me and I trusted him. He wouldn't judge me and reject me. He wouldn't care that I was old and fat. He'd see me as his friend and maybe we could start all over again.

We would just pick up where we had left off. I needed someone to wrap his arms around me and comfort me. So I called him.

I'm sure that I scared him to death. Before, when we had been together, we were on equal ground. Both of us had been married to someone we loved and there was an unspoken understanding that neither of us would ever leave our spouses. Now the circumstances had changed. I was alone and needy. He made it quite clear that he was more than willing to start seeing me again whenever it was possible, but I could tell that he was afraid that I might want more than he was capable of giving. Had the situation been reversed, I would have felt the same way. The risk of being exposed was now a reality that he was unwilling to take.

One day, just before the kids and I moved, Jim stopped by at lunch to see me. He came in and sat down and our dog was immediately at my feet begging for attention. I turned to her and said, "It's okay, honey. I love you too. Don't be jealous. I'll always love you, you know that." When I looked up at him, he had the strangest look on his face. I asked him what was the matter and he said, "You've said those same words to me."

I didn't think much about it, at the time, but as I have made my way through my struggle of self discovery over the past few years, I can now see what a revelation that was. He was right. I had said those very same words to him before when we would talk about Steve. I had probably said it to Steve and Kym and Sean and Brittany, too. I loved everyone the same. Husbands, lovers, siblings, children and, yes, even pets. I loved everyone who would let me love them. My entire life revolved around making sure everyone knew how much I loved them. It was the same old story. I had to make sure I loved everyone as much as I could so that they would never feel unloved like that little girl that lived inside of me.

Fortunately for both of us, I moved away soon after that and the distance made it easier for me to stay away from him. I gained a lot of weight and I think that maybe, subconsciously, it was my way of protecting myself from my own weaknesses. Believe you me, there is no doubt in my mind that on days when I was weak, and there were many, if I hadn't been so fat, I'd have been on the phone trying to figure out someway for us to get together. The weight was my protection. It saved me from myself until I had the strength to do it myself.

I was alone in a new city with no friends or family. I was very depressed and so desperately wanted someone to comfort me. I was lonely and vulnerable and confused. Steve was gone and I needed someone to hold me and tell me everything would be all right. Before I started this journey, I would have called Jim and never thought twice about whether or not it was right or wrong, but I was determined to break my old habits. Despite my new determination, there were still days when I struggled to do what was right and I asked God to help me stay strong.

The support I was looking for came just in the nick of time. I was watching television and Oprah came on and her guest was Iyanla Vanzant, who was promoting her book "Yesterday I Cried." She had been on the show before and she was a marvelous speaker. She was very spiritual and her mission was to help people, women in particular, to tap into their own strengths and improve not only their emotional, but also their spiritual well being.

She was talking about how she had experienced low self-esteem and had let herself be mistreated by men. She had been emotionally abandoned by her father and had used sexual relationships with the wrong men to try and fill the void she felt inside. As she was describing her struggle to find herself beneath all the garbage that life had dumped on her, I thought about how similar our lives had been.

Of course, I went out the next day and bought her book and, in my usual obsessive manner, read it from front to back in 48 hours. We were two woman sent to Earth for almost the exact same experience. We had lived the first part of our lives in a frenzied, impulsive manner, making mistake after mistake in order to learn all the lessons we would need to complete the second half of our lives. We were both destined to become strong women who would write and speak about struggle and survival.

There were a lot of differences, too. For starters, she was African American and I was Caucasian. Her mother had died when she was a child and mine had not. She had been physically abused and I had not. The biggest difference was that her soul mate had come into her life to help her with the second part of her journey and was giving her great joy while she was far enough along to realize why he was sent to her. Steve had come into my life during the first part of my journey and had given me great joy, but it wasn't until after he was gone that I began to grow spiritually and truly understand and appreciate why he had come to me.

Many days, in my weakest moments, as I struggled with my need to be loved at any cost, I needed divine guidance. God had once again sent it to me through Oprah, in the shape of this beautiful, honest woman. This is a direct quote from her book …..

"I found myself doing with him what I had done in the past. I was trying to make him change his mind. I was sleeping with a man who was not giving me all that I wanted and needed. And I was using a relationship as the barometer by which I measured my success. When we were on, I was on. When he didn't call or come over, I felt like everything was falling apart. He brought up all of my worth issues, my abandonment issues, and he helped me to see that I was still looking for love "out there." Once I realized what I was doing, I didn't have the strength or courage to stop. I kept seeing him for more than a year before I remembered the list. **What do you want?** I want a man who is willing to be seen with me in public. **What is your greatest fear?** That I will never find a man to love me. **What is your greatest weakness?** Needing someone to love me. **Why?** Because I don't love myself. **Why?** Because I'm not good enough. **Why?** Because that is what I have been told. Each time I worked with the list, new questions and deeper insights emerged. I never said a word to my friend. I just stopped calling. So did he. When he did call, months later, I was well on my way to learning "I am the love I seek."

That could have been me talking. That was where I was headed. The message was loud and clear: I didn't need this man to love me. I needed to love myself.

Steve's words from when we were first dating came back to me, "You're too good to waste your time on a man who belongs to someone else." He was right then and he was right now. He was screaming down from Heaven trying to get me to hear him. I knew right then and there that I would never again share any man with another woman, even if it meant that I would be without a partner for the rest of my life.

It had been a long, depressing winter. Along with the weight I had gained , I had also gained a lot of knowledge. I realize that it was something that I had to go through in order to grow, but it was one of the darkest times of my life.

Sometime during the first two months of 1999, our house back home finally sold. I had changed realtors after three months of little or no activity and now my new realtor was telling me that maybe I was asking too much for it. I, however, was determined to stick to my guns. That house was my hope for a brighter future. Most of my inheritance from Steve was tied up in his 401(k) and I couldn't touch it for many years without taking a huge tax hit. I needed to make enough off of the sale of the house to assure me that we would be able to buy a decent home in which we could start over.

I prayed every night when I went to bed for the house to sell. The lease was almost up on our apartment and I was spending a lot of money on rent. I asked God to please take this problem from me. I didn't care how He did it, but I needed to get out from under this burden and get on with our lives.

Just when I was about to give in and lower the price, the market broke and I had several offers come in all at the same time. I accepted the highest one, which was exactly what I had hoped to get for it. Could it be that this turning things over to God thing actually worked? Was it really that simple? Just ask Him to take it and He would?

I was so excited to finally start looking for a new home. I called a local realtor and told her that I was looking for a house out in the country. I asked for three bedrooms, a two-car garage, a fireplace and either a pond or a creek. Sean loved to fish and I wanted him to have some place on our property to fish so I wouldn't have to drive him to a lake all the time.

She called me the next day and said that she had found absolutely nothing in my price range with a pond or a creek on the property. She said that she had never even seen anything close to my require-ments during the many years she had been a realtor, but she assured me that she would keep trying.

Just for fun, I got on the internet and looked up a real estate site and plugged in all the details and there it was — "our house." A little over two acres of land out in the country with a house that had three bedrooms, a two-car garage and not only did it have a stocked pond in the back yard, but it also had a meandering creek flowing through the property. I couldn't believe my eyes. It didn't have a fireplace and it was all electric, but I didn't care. I called the realtor and she looked it up and told me that there was already an offer out on it, but that she would let me know if by some "miracle" it fell through.

A couple of weeks went by and I still hadn't heard from her. I had pretty much given up hope that my "miracle" would actually happen.

My brother, Scott, lives not too far from us and his wife's family raises horses which they race at a local harness racing track. Sean and Brittany had been bugging me to go see the horses for a while and I finally agreed. Scott came and picked us up because I didn't know the area very well yet. I had told him about the house I had found on the internet and, as we were driving down the road that the horse barn was on, he said, "Hey, that house that you told me about is right down that street. Do you want to drive past it?" Well, of course, I said yes. As soon as I saw it I knew it was the house we were supposed to buy.

That night, as I settled down to sleep, I prayed, "God, I want that house. I'm turning it over to you. If we get it great and if not I'll understand, but I just wanted to let you know my wishes and ask for your guidance."

Not too long after that, the realtor called to say that the deal had, amazingly, fallen through and she set up a time for us to go see it.

The house needed some work, but I knew I wanted to raise Sean and Brittany there. Before I knew it, it was almost March and we were getting ready to move into our new house.

I had to tear up all the carpet because the people who lived there before us had ten cats. I had all the walls painted to get rid of years of cigarette smoke and the kitchen appliances were very old and dark so I replaced them all with white to brighten things up a bit. There was no basement so I had a construction company come and build a room above the garage for the kids to use as a play room. When everything was done, it was exactly what we needed and I was quite pleased with myself.

There was a small barn connected to the garage where the boy who lived there before kept his llama. The woman took five of her cats and asked if she could leave the other five with us. I was never much of a cat fancier, but I gave in to Brittany's pleas to keep them. I insisted, however, that they remain outside in the barn. After all, Sean had brought his dog, Lucky, with us when we moved and Brittany had been begging for a pet of her own.

For a little while, I was so busy that I didn't have the time or the energy to feel depressed or try to find out answers to my many questions about Steve's death or even think about what life held in store for me. I was actually feeling tiny sparks of happiness.

My momentary happiness was interrupted as I realized that March 14th was approaching and it would soon be a whole year since Steve had died. So much had happened in that year that I couldn't believe that the time had passed so quickly. My pain was not as severe, but I still cried at the drop of a hat and longed to be comforted. I decided to plan a memorial mass back home for Steve. I wrote two letters to put in the local paper. The first was from a Kenny Rogers song that made me think of Steve and what he would say to Sean and Brittany if he could talk to them:

Sean and Brittany,

I promise you
Whatever I do
You are the most important thing to me
I give my word
I will be heard
No one will ever take you from me
And when you close your eyes
Know I will always come to you
And part of me will always be right there next to you
Someday there'll be
Just wait and see
Somewhere a place for you and me

Love, Daddy

The second one was from me to Steve and read like this:

In Loving Memory of
Stephen C. Donatini
May 13, 1950 - March 14, 1998

So many times during the past year, I have wondered if maybe losing you would have been less painful if only I hadn't loved you so much. Last week, as I was driving down the road, God answered my question. I turned on Sean's Garth Brooks CD and these words came out to speak to me:

"Looking back on the memory of
the dance we shared beneath the stars above.
For a moment all the world was right

142

but how could I have known you'd ever say goodbye.
And, now, I'm glad I didn't know the way it all would end,
the way it all would go.
Our lives are better left to chance.
I could have missed the pain
but I'd of had to miss the dance."

I miss you so much! The pain goes on, but having you in my life for even just one moment was worth it all!

Thanks for the dance!

I will love you forever.

Kathy

(A memorial mass to celebrate Steve's life will be held at St. Joan of Arc Parish on Sunday, March 14, 1999 at 10:30 a.m. for those of you who wish to attend.)

That week, as we were getting our things ready to go back home for the mass, Brittany asked me if I thought that Grandma Donatini and Aunt Lynn would see the articles in the paper and come to the mass. I told her that they might, but not to count on it. I asked her why she wanted to know and her answer surprised me. She said, "I miss them, Grandma, and I wish you would make up with them so we could see them again."

All night long, I lay in bed and thought about what she had said. Was I being selfish and only thinking of myself? Sean and Brittany had lost so much — Steve, Kym, their friends, their house. Could I swallow my pride and call and ask them to come to the mass so that Brittany could see them? I loved Brittany, but I wasn't sure I wanted to talk to them, so I called when I thought they might not be home. I left a message on Lynn's answering machine telling her about the memorial mass saying that Brittany wanted me to call and invite them.

It was a very emotional day for us. Father Dyer was there and my sister and her family came to be with us, as well as many dear friends. I had asked them to play a song that they played at Steve's funeral called "On Eagle's Wings" and tears flowed from my eyes as the song brought back sad memories:

And He will raise you up on eagle's wings,
bear you on the breath of dawn,
make you to shine just like the sun,
and hold you in the palm of His hand.

God certainly was holding us in the palm of His hand that day for, at that very moment, Brittany's little face lit up and she squealed with joy, "Look Grandma and Aunt Lynn are here." When they walked past me after they took communion, they both touched my shoulder gently to make sure that I had seen them. Brittany could hardly contain herself until the end of the mass when she ran outside to see if they were still there. She came scurrying back in and told me to hurry because Grandma Pauline, Lynn, Dave and Dino were waiting for us outside. I told Pauline we were going to go get something to eat and stop by the cemetery and she asked if she could go with us. We spent a nice afternoon together and the healing began.

We see each other often now and I have to say that Pauline and I are close and have a loving relationship. We have talked about what happened and she has never attempted to give me an explanation for their actions. When I tried to explain my feelings to her, she said that she understood and that she still thinks that I just had lost my mind. Lynn and her family try their best to treat us like we are a part of the family. Although I no longer need them to love me, it is nice when sometimes they act as though they do.

One day shortly after that, while both the kids were at school, my sister-in-law, Leasa, came over to see the house and we had a house warming ceremony. She is very spiritual and follows many Native American customs and she burnt some sage and asked the spirits to bless our new house.

I told her how desperately I needed to know that Steve could hear me when I spoke to him. I asked her if she could help me learn to talk to him. He had died so suddenly that I didn't get to tell him about something that I had done and I needed to ask him to forgive me.

She said, "You don't need to learn to talk to him. Just talk to him. He will hear you." She explained to me that whatever it was that I had done, she was certain that he had forgiven me already because once you die and go to the other side, you let go of all your earthly ego issues. She said that she felt fairly certain that he knew about or, at least suspected, what I had done prior to his death.

I started to try to explain the affair to her and I made a feeble attempt to explain why I had done the things I had. In her own direct fashion, she taught me a wonderful lesson about the word "justification." She said that I needed to start accepting responsibility for my actions. She suggested that I try to stop justifying everything and just admit it when I was wrong and make an effort to live at a higher level of consciousness. She reminded me that everyone makes mistakes, but it is not the mistakes themselves that matter. It is whether or not you learn from your mistakes. She told me that I already had Steve's forgiveness and that now what I really needed to do was forgive myself. Before I could forgive myself, I had to admit that what I had done was a choice I had made and I had to accept responsibility for it without trying to justify it.

I remember once on our anniversary Steve saying to me "I can't believe it. We've been married all these years and I've never been with any one else." I answered, "I know that and it means a lot to me." The response I should have been able to say was "Me neither," but it would have been a lie. In my heart, I felt guilty and wanted to confess to him that I had been with someone else. Maybe, subconsciously, I wanted him to find out but, in reality, I was afraid that, if I told him, he would leave me. Rather than risk the worst, I took the easy way out and said nothing. I thought about confessing to a priest. Maybe that would ease my pain. I searched through Sean and Brittany's CCD instruction books trying to see what the Catholic church had to say about adultery. I wasn't raised in the Catholic church and I wanted to see what the commandment "Thou shalt not commit adultery" really meant. Somehow, I needed to "justify" my actions. Maybe, I would be able to turn that commandment around some way so that it would fit my situation.

Before I understood why I had been unfaithful, I had all kinds of reasons why I had done it. Steve wasn't romantic enough. He never told me he loved me. He was always too tired to help me or even listen to me. I was always helping him, but he never thought about what I needed. He wouldn't talk to me about things. He wouldn't even fight with me. He just shut me out. At the time, they all sounded like good reasons to turn to someone else.

Once, I had even written him a long letter and told him how much I missed the man I had married. I even suggested that we go to counseling. I needed him to be my husband again and not just

146

my roommate. I don't know what his response to the letter was because he never mentioned it after he read it. That was how he dealt with uncomfortable situations, just pretend like nothing had ever happened.

I always believed that someday I would tell him about the affair. Maybe when we were really old and it wouldn't be such a big deal, but we didn't get old together. I never imagined he'd go into a coma suddenly one night while I was at home sleeping and we'd never get to talk to each other again before he died.

There are many things I do differently now that I have gone through this whole ordeal, but I think one of the most profound changes in how I live my life is that I have no secrets. If there is something that I have done or something that I feel, I discuss it truthfully with the person or people that it impacts. Regret is something I never want to experience again.

I thought about what Leasa had said and decided that I might feel less guilty if I could muster up the courage to admit what I had done out loud to someone. This was very risky and it would have to be someone safe.

The next day I called Monica, knowing that she wouldn't judge me. I hemmed and hawed around for what seemed like forever. I don't think I actually told her any details, but I'm sure she got the message I was trying to convey. She was her wonderful understanding self, which I am sure was difficult for her because her first husband had an affair and married the other woman after they divorced. She had made it very clear to me on numerous occasions over the years that adultery was not something that she could tolerate or accept.

I don't know what I was expecting, but I didn't feel any less guilty after we hung up. I wasn't sure that there would ever be anything

I could do that would take it away. I was sure that the punishment for my sin was going to be living the rest of my life with this terrible guilt hanging over me.

I turned on Oprah and there was some guy named Phil McGraw talking to a guest. Oprah called him "Tell-it-like-it-is Phil." The show was about people who had been hurt terribly by someone else and they wanted the other person to say they were sorry.

Dr. Phil was promoting his new book, "Life Strategies," and he was going through a list of "Life Laws" which he suggested you use to help you get through life's tough spots. I don't remember all ten of them, but the ones that stuck with me were these:

You need to be accountable for your life.
You can't change what you don't acknowledge.
You have to name it to claim it.
There is power in forgiveness.

As I watched the show, I had what Oprah calls one of those "light bulb" moments. These people were sitting there saying how sorry they were, but they couldn't just let it go at that. They had to add the infamous "but" to their apologies. You know what I mean. I'm sorry, "but" it wasn't my fault. They all blamed it on their past or said that it was actually the other person's fault because of how they had treated them. They were all trying to "justify" their actions in order to make themselves feel better about what they had done. No one wanted to own up to their wrongdoings.

They were doing just what I had been doing that day with Leasa.

Finally, Dr. Phil got furious with one woman and he shouted at her, "Look, you either get it or you don't. And, lady, you just don't get it."

Wham, it hit me right between the eyes. Finally, what Leasa had been trying to tell me hit home. I hadn't been getting it.

What I had done was terrible. It was wrong. Steve trusted me and I broke that trust. I was being selfish and only thinking of myself. I'm sure that, at the time, I felt that there was a perfectly good reason for my unfaithfulness and there might even have been things from my past that led up to my decision to be unfaithful, but the bottom line was that there was no justification for it. What I had done was wrong and it was time to accept responsibility for my actions. It was time to be truthful for the first time in my life and stop blaming all my problems on someone else. I had other options and "I" chose not to use them.

It wasn't my mother who had made the decision to have an affair. It wasn't my father or my first love or my first husband. It was me and me alone. I had spent my entire life doing what made me feel good for the moment even though I knew it was wrong. Then I tried to "justify" it in my mind. I just never got it — until that very moment.

Leasa had explained to me that Steve had forgiven me and I didn't need God's forgiveness because he would never judge me in the first place. So, why then was I still feeling like there was something else I needed to do in order to let go of my guilt?

I remembered Dr. Phil saying, "What would happen if you forgave yourself?" I thought for a while and realized that I still needed to forgive myself. I remember saying out loud, "Yeah, that sounds so easy, but how do I do that?"

I always taped the Oprah show so that I could replay the parts that really hit home. So, later that night, after the kids went to sleep, I watched the show again and I fast forwarded to the part where Dr. Phil had talked about forgiveness. He said, "Once you let go of the emotional attachment and forgive yourself, it will no longer control you. It won't be easy. You'll have to work on it every day because life is managed, not cured."

I sat on the couch with tears dripping off my chin and I forgave myself that night. I've had to do it many, many times over the past few years because sometimes I forget and start backsliding, but that's all part of "managing" it.

I've been told that there are no accidents in life. That there are no such things as coincidences. Everything happens for a reason, just exactly as it has been planned.

I have always been an avid reader. In the first grade, while the rest of the class was reading the "See Jerry Run" books, I was reading Doctor Doolittle. I would read anything I could get my hands on — newspapers, magazines, even pamphlets lying on the counter at the teller window in the bank. When Steve and I went on vacation, I always took two or three books to read. It drove him crazy. All I had to do to make him pay attention to me was pick up a book. I often felt as though he thought of my books as competition. Once, a friend of ours actually had a T-shirt made up that said "Not Now Steve, I'm Reading" and I took it with me on vacation as a joke.

It wasn't unusual for me to pamper myself by spending hours at Barnes & Noble just browsing through the shelves in search of something interesting to read. On one particular morning, it was as if I was being pulled into the store on my way home from dropping Sean and Brittany off at school.

I wandered around the self-help section, the new age section, the children's section, but nothing jumped out and grabbed me. Then lying there on a table in the center of an aisle were books by an author named Wayne Dyer. I had never heard of him, but I picked up one of the books and read the cover and flipped through it. It seemed to be a motivational book, something about manifesting your destiny. It sounded too new age for me. It was getting late and I had grocery shopping to do so I left the store without buying anything.

The next week, I got a flyer in the mail from a book club and there was that name again, Wayne Dyer. It was advertising a book called "Your Sacred Self." I read the write up and, once again, I didn't think I would like the book.

This was obviously an author whose books I was supposed to read because that weekend our local PBS station was running a lecture by Wayne Dyer. It was late at night and I couldn't sleep so I decided maybe I'd listen to this Wayne Dyer guy and see what he had to say.

If you have ever listened to Wayne Dyer speak, you already know that he is an exceptional speaker. His voice is very appealing and he speaks to you as if he were your friend. He tells humorous stories and shares very personal aspects of his life with his audience and makes you feel as if you have known him forever. Listening to him lecture is a very enjoyable experience .

The powers that be were using every trick in the book to get their message across to me. First Leasa, then Dr. Phil and now Wayne Dyer.

He spoke about many wonderful theories. How you have to be careful what you think because your thoughts affect what happens to you. Negative thoughts going out attract negative circumstances coming back into your life. He said that through the use of positive thoughts and intentions you could actually create a better life for yourself and "manifest your own destiny." I have to say that I

151

enjoyed the show very much. It started me thinking about things I had never even considered before.

Not too long after that, I was once again treating myself to a trip to Barnes & Noble looking for tapes to play in the car during my long rides home to visit our family and friends. The trip takes about four hours and Sean and Brittany always put on their headphones and listen to their music on their CD players. This gave me the rare opportunity to actually have the tape player to myself. I had found that listening to old tapes from when Steve was alive usually brought back memories connected to the songs. Even though the memories were wonderful, the pain was still too fresh and I would inevitably end up crying, which upset the kids — not to mention the fact that it made it hard to see where I was going. I decided to look for books on tape to help pass these long hours on the road.

I bought three or four of Mr. Dyer's tapes and have listened to them all so many times that they surely will break someday from overuse. One of the tapes, entitled "Living Without Limits" by Wayne Dyer and a gentleman named Deepak Chopra, was exceptionally moving and I really enjoyed it. These two men had a very obvious connection and they really complimented one another. Mr. Chopra spoke with a thick Indian accent and Mr. Dyer teased him about it on the tape. His voice mesmerized me and the next time I was in Barnes & Noble, I bought another audio cassette by Deepak Chopra entitled "The Seven Spiritual Laws of Success," which finalized my lesson on "justification."

I won't even try to write exactly the words that Mr. Chopra said in his message, but it was something like this: Every person must make decisions in his or her life. No matter how hard you might try not to, you still must make choices. Even if it is only as simple as choosing whether or not to be offended by something that someone says to you or, for that matter, whether or not you choose to be flattered by a compliment someone gives you. You actually make many decisions every day without even consciously knowing it.

He went on to explain that, before he makes any decision in his life, he asks himself two questions. First, "What are the possible consequences of this decision?" and second, "Will this decision bring joy and fulfillment to me and those closest to me?" He said that, by simply asking himself these two questions, every decision in his life is very easy for him to make. He said that we cannot make our decisions based on what feels good at that moment. We must raise ourselves to a higher level of consciousness. We must do what is best for everyone concerned because we are all connected. What we do affects not only ourselves but the entire universe.

I had once again been taught a very valuable lesson. One that has finally eased my pain. When things were going wrong in our marriage and I didn't get the response from Steve that I needed, I'd had a decision to make and I decided to do what made me feel good at the moment. In doing so, I threw the stone into the pond and, as the ripple spread out to the edges, it touched the lives of many other people. I thought of this as "my own business," but there is no such thing.

I now know that everything I do affects the entire universe, so I must start making wiser decisions. It had taken many years of suffering to learn this lesson, but maybe nothing less would have done. Maybe I had to experience loss and guilt of this magnitude in order to learn not to put my needs, wants and comforts first.

There was no doubt that what I had done was terrible, but I no longer felt guilty about it. I had finally forgiven myself. I felt deep, sincere regret, but the guilt was gone. I finally saw the lesson. The powers that be had to go to some effort to get it through to me, but finally I "got it." I was not in this world for me alone. I had a connection with the entire universe and I would never again forget to see the big picture.

Right after all these lessons had been presented to me, I got a call from my sister saying that my mom was in the hospital. She had surgery on her colon earlier in the week and she wasn't doing so well. My mom had always been a hypochondriac. Whenever she got sick, we all took it with a grain of salt, but this time Margie seemed to be genuinely concerned and said that maybe my brother, Scott, and I should try to come home.

Scott called and asked me if he could catch a ride with us so that he wouldn't have to drive all that way alone. I was thrilled to have an adult to travel with and, of course, said "yes." I talked his ear off for the entire four-hour trip home telling him about all my messages from above. Sean and Brittany put their headphones on after awhile because they couldn't bear to listen to me go on and on any longer. Not Scott, he not only listened, but he seemed to be genuinely interested.

Scott and I had never been what you would call close when we were growing up. He was ten years younger and had always been a quiet person. The things I remember most about him were that he played football in high school and Kym and I went to watch him play. He got married to his high school sweetheart and was the first of my siblings to move away from our hometown.

He was the type of person that always wanted everyone to get along. When my youngest brother had broken ties with my parents, he tried to get them to patch things up. When he and his first wife got divorced, he wrote this beautiful letter and put it in with his Christmas card asking all of us to please remember that, no matter what may have gone on between the two of them, she would always be a part of his family because of their two children. He said that her family still treated him as one of the family and that he hoped that we could find it in our hearts to do the same.

I'm sure that part of the reason I was guided to live closer to him was so that I could get to know him better. Having him and his new family close by made life much easier, but, more importantly, he and Leasa have both helped me to learn what it means to truly believe in a higher power.

While we were home, complications arose from mom's surgery and it became fairly obvious that she probably wasn't going to make it. They told us that the next few days would be crucial. I was going to just stay, but we had been there since Wednesday and the kids had already missed two days of school. Scott needed to get back to work and we made a joint decision to head back home. We could come back, if need be, once we saw how things went over the next few days.

On the way back, we talked about everything: growing up, mom and dad, kids, spouses, life and death. As I listened to him talk, I realized how truly spiritual he was. He explained things to me in a way I had never heard before. He answered the question I had asked when I read "Embraced By The Light." He said that the reason I didn't know about all this sooner was because if I had known I wouldn't have learned the lessons I needed to learn.

He told me that he had always known, maybe not on a conscious level, but somewhere deep down inside him. He said that marrying Leasa had helped him to let the knowledge that had always been there rise to the surface.

Here is the message he gave me: "Everyone has a choice of using a higher power or not using it and going through life alone. If we go it alone, we become exhausted and have unhappy outcomes, but if we ask for the help of God, we tap into the source of all love and wisdom. God will give us the guidance and energy to do whatever we need to do." He said that now that he knows, it is hard to hold back when someone doesn't understand. He wants to tell everyone he meets that not choosing God is doing things the hard way and that when you see the whole picture things make so much more sense.

I am very blessed to have him as a brother. I love him with all my heart and am eternally grateful to him for sharing his wisdom with me.

℘ *Peace* ℘

Before we knew it Thanksgiving and Christmas had once again come and gone and it was the beginning of a new millennium. In three more months, it would be two years since Steve had died. Just as everyone had said, time was beginning to heal my pain. Every day I was getting stronger.

The kids were back at school after Christmas break and I was looking for something productive to do. I decided to pull out Steve's medical files again and see where I had left off.

When Monica looked over the files for me a year earlier, she had mentioned that they thought it might be something called sarcoidosis and I had looked it up on the internet and found a local support group. When I called the woman in charge of the group, she referred me to a local hospital that was doing some research on sarcoidosis. I called the head of the department and was told that, although they studied the disease, they really weren't in the practice of reviewing medical files. They gave me the name of a doctor who specialized in sarcoidosis who they thought might be involved in performing that type of review.

He was very helpful and told me that without an autopsy he couldn't be sure whether or not Steve had actually suffered from sarcoidosis. He also stated that, to his knowledge, there was no evidence linking the development of lung cancer to patients having been diagnosed with sarcoidosis. He said he was sorry he couldn't be of more help, but he thought maybe I was searching for an answer that just wasn't there.

At that point, I had pretty much decided to just let it go. Since we had moved into the new house, I always had other things to keep my mind occupied. I was volunteering at the school a couple of days a week and I was trying to figure out how to come to terms with all the changes in my life.

I decided that maybe the last doctor was right and that I wouldn't be able to get the answers I longed for so desperately. I took the files and stuck them back in the drawer and decided maybe I had better try cleaning the garage or something instead.

A few days later, out of the blue, Monica called me and told me that she had found a copy of an article about a possible link between sarcoidosis and lung cancer that was being researched in Italy. She had gone to use the copier and someone had obviously walked away and left their original on the glass. She felt that it wasn't just a coincidence that she found it and said she was going to mail it to me.

I called the specialist back and asked him if he felt that this might change his opinion about his review of Steve's files. He hesitated for a moment and then he told me that he had a feeling that he hadn't heard the last of me. When he talked to me the last time, he had almost told me about something that he had found in the pathology report from Steve's open lung biopsy. He said that pathology wasn't his field, but I might want to read the comments at the bottom of the report and perhaps have someone in that specialty explain it to me. He really didn't want to say much more, but he wished me luck and said goodbye.

After we hung up, I went and got the report and it said, "Based upon the findings of our special stains, we favor poorly differentiated adenocarcinoma with lymphangiectic type of metastasis. Differential diagnosis will include testicular neoplasm, particularly embryonal carcinoma with choriocarcinomatous trait."

I couldn't believe my eyes. This explained so much. If Steve had testicular cancer, it was no wonder he had become impotent and that he was having pain in his testicles when he coughed. If the cancer had begun to spread to his lungs, that would explain why he had been coughing nonstop for the past six months. Finally, I might have the answer to how he had gotten lung cancer.

Why hadn't anyone ever told me this before? The doctors at the hospital, the pulmonary specialist, Dr. Keller, the doctor who I had paid to review the file way back in June of 1998, none of them ever once mentioned anything to me that the lungs were not the primary source of the cancer. This report seemed to indicate that the pathology report favored testicular neoplasm as the primary source.

I decided to try and find a pathologist who would agree to examine the lung biopsy slides to see what he thought. After several unsuccessful attempts, I finally reached a wonderful gentleman who agreed to review the slides. He suggested that I work through an attorney just in case we ever decided to use the results of his review in court. His initial report, which was based on slides from the hospital where Steve had died, was that there was a malignant tumor in the lung the was most likely a metastatic germ cell tumor. However, he needed more tissue in order to determine whether or not it was embryonic carcinoma of the testes.

Fortunately for me, we were able to obtain a block of tissue that was still on file at the hospital and sent it to him for review. The results indicated that Steve's cancer favored germ cell tumor over lung carcinoma. Bingo! We were finally getting somewhere.

A radiologist also confirmed that there was no evidence of medi- astinal germ cell tumor to suggest a primary mediastinal tumor and that he believed it was extra thoracic in origin. In layman's terms, he agreed with the pathologist.

Next a cancer specialist reviewed the files and said that the form of cancer Steve had occurs in approximately 7,500 patients a year in the United States and is curable about 75% of the time. He said the tumor was fast growing and had been know to double in as little as 28 days. The part that really floored me was when he said that he felt that had Steve been diagnosed even 21 days earlier, effective treat- ment could have saved his life. He was surprised that the symptoms of progressive, unremitting cough for almost a 12-month duration prior to his death did not persuade Steve's physician that a chest x-ray might have been useful prior to 19 days before his death.

Finally, after two years, I not only knew what had caused Steve's death, but I had been told that it was avoidable. If Dr. Keller had used what is referred to in medical terms as "normal community standards of care," Steve might have never died.

I have found out since then that there was a large mass in Steve's liver that looked suspicious that they were going to do a biopsy on next. However, that never happened because he died before they had a chance to run the tests. Maybe he had chronic hepatitis, not diabetes, the entire time I knew him, which caused liver cancer, which spread to the testes and then to the lungs and who knows where else.

I had known all along that there was something that I hadn't been told, but I never expected it to be this devastating. It was unbelievable to me that not one single doctor out of all those involved in Steve's final days had the integrity to tell me the truth. I had just wanted to understand what had really happened. I was simply trying to come to terms with not having an autopsy done. I needed answers to the questions that had never been answered. I never expected to uncover this heartbreaking information. I'm sure that none of them ever expected me to figure it out either. Now, after all this time, I finally understood why the pulmonary specialist wrote to Dr. Keller the day after Steve died and told him that there had not been an autopsy done. I would imagine that they were both relieved.

People who have nothing to hide, hide nothing. Guilt by omission is just as bad as out and out lying. Take it from someone who knows. I speak from personal experience.

Did Dr. Keller know this all along? Was that what he meant that day in his office when he said he couldn't believe that he had missed it? How many other families go on living with these same doubts after the death of a loved one never knowing what really happened — trusting that the doctors are telling them the truth? Mistakes are expected, but what if the doctor wasn't giving his patients the quality of care to which they were entitled? What if their trust was undeserved and this was just a job to him — just a way to make money? What if keeping the HMO happy by keeping costs down was more important than the well being of your patient? Isn't this where the Hippocratic Oath comes in? Isn't there something in there about "first do no harm?"

After all my spiritual growth, could I put into action what I claimed to believe —that we are all one and, therefore, should think of the interest of all people and not just ourselves? What was my responsibility in this situation? Whose loved one would be next? What if it were someone I knew? Even if it wasn't, hadn't I just decided that everyone was equally important to me. I kept talking about how we were all connected. Could I allow myself to just walk away in silence and pretend that it didn't matter? It would be very painful to go through a lawsuit which could drag on for years and delay the closure I longed for and deserved. Did I have what it would take to go up against the "good old boy" system? Could I walk the walk or was it all just lip service? I had already spent thousands of dollars getting this far and it could cost me a lot more to bring this to Dr. Keller's attention. Was I ready to practice what I preached and say that money wasn't as important as doing the right thing. It's possible that all that would happen was that Dr. Keller would be made aware of what I had uncovered in my search for answers. He might deny it and learn nothing from it. Would it be enough to see it through to the end and feel some pride in knowing that I had done everything that I could?

I decided I would turn it over to God. I'd been doing a lot of that lately and it seemed to be working just fine. I prayed that night for guidance. If I was supposed to pursue this, I would be His messenger. If not, I would accept the results of my years of searching for answers and be satisfied with simply finally knowing what had really happened. Then I patiently sat back and waited for my answer.

My life was getting easier and easier. I was keeping my eyes open and watching for messages that were being sent to help me know what direction I was supposed to be going in next. I was feeling much better about everything, but I found myself feeling guilty if I went out somewhere and actually enjoyed myself. I still hadn't given myself permission to be happy again.

I had been trying to tackle a book that I had bought a long time ago called "A Course In Miracles." It would be an understatement to say that I was totally overwhelmed by what I was reading. I am sure that the "Course" would have helped me immensely, but I just couldn't find the discipline to sit down and do the required exercises. I kept trying, but was met with little success.

Then I found a set of tapes by a woman named Marianne Williamson that were based on "A Course In Miracles" and I decided that maybe it would be easier to listen to what someone else had to say about it. Marianne Williamson is one of America's foremost interpreters of "A Course In Miracles" and had struggled most of her life prior to finding her answers to life's mysteries in the Course. She is a wonderful speaker who adds humor to her lectures and brings the messages down to a level that makes them understandable to even the most undisciplined of us.

I listened to the first set and went out and bought several more tapes, but my favorite, by far, was one entitled "Hope and The Choice To Be Happy." In it she explains how to move beyond your past mistakes and encourages the listener to not get stuck in guilt and self-judgment. She says that all you have to do is ask God to heal you of your past through a process called Atonement, which she describes as an "undoing."

Here is a short version of this process: We all make mistakes. If we were already perfect, we wouldn't be here. When you make a mistake, you can choose to pretend it didn't happen, blame it on someone or something else, feel guilty and judge yourself (which just keeps the cycle going), or you can face what you did, analyze why you did it and "chose not to do it again." That doesn't mean that it wasn't something that you wished you hadn't done. It means that you did it, you realize that it was not a loving thing to do and you are now choosing to act differently from this day forward.

Remember the song from Sunday school that went "This little light of mine. I'm gonna' let it shine?" Marianne Williamson taught me that there is a light in all of us when we are born. Mine had just gotten very small — almost diminished. She reminded me that I am a child of God and that I have a responsibility to the universe to "shine" as brightly as I possibly can.

She says that suffering can, indeed, be a transformative experience, but that happiness can also be transformative and a lot more fun. She challenged me to let go of my suffering and make more room for happiness in every part of my life. I had changed myself internally and it was time for me to change my external world to match that "light" that I had re-ignited in my soul.

Happiness is a decision we make. I didn't have to suffer in order to be spiritual. I needed to give myself permission to be happy again. I had forgiven myself for my mistakes, but I was still punishing myself by not allowing my life to be joyous and fulfilling.

I still haven't done "The Course In Miracles." Maybe I never will, but, with the help of Marianne Williamson, I had given myself permission to start being happy again.

One day shortly after this lesson in "happiness," I called my sister to ask her something and her husband, John, answered and told me that she was at a funeral. Although Margie and John have been married for many years and she and I have been known to talk each others ear off, I very rarely spoke at any length with John. Something in the sound of his voice made me think that he might be upset and need to talk to someone. We made the usual small talk and then he told me that he had just hung up the phone from a call telling him that his Aunt Jo had passed away. I made an attempt at comforting him and somehow the conversation turned from dying to God and eternity.

He said that in the overall scheme of things, he was certain that our time on Earth was but a blink of an eye compared to what followed. He said that occasionally when he stopped after work to have a drink with his buddies, they would talk about religion. He told me that some of these guys had questioned God's existence because they couldn't believe that a real God would let terrible things happen to innocent people. He said he never really knew what to tell them and we sort of let it go at that.

That night I lay in bed and pondered the question we hadn't answered. If there really is a God, why does He let horrible things happen to us? To my amazement, I realized that I knew the answer. Maybe not everyone's answer, but certainly one that made sense to me. It gave me a great deal of comfort to understand this long unanswered mystery.

Over the past two years, I had read every book I could get my hands on to help me understand this force that I call God. I know that not everyone believes in my God. Different cultures and different religions each have their own beliefs. I chose God because He is who I was raised to believe in as a child. Call it what you want.

The choice is up to you. I could have used some "new age" word like "a higher power," but I needed to be authentic and, for me, the word is God.

I read the Celestine Prophecy series, many books by the Dalai Lama, the Conversations with God series and, of course, all the books I've mentioned throughout this book. I bought an audio tape of The Bible and played it in the car when I would drive back and forth to pick up the kids from school. Then, of course, there was Oprah and her spiritual guests. I wanted to be sure I was seeing things from every perspective.

What an informative two years it had been. Some of it must have sunk in because here I was coming up with an answer to John's unanswered question.

God is not a mean, punishing, judgmental God. He is a loving, compassionate God whose only wish for His children is for them to love one another. He allows us to visit this world and experience certain things in order to help us rise to a higher level of spirituality and return Home where we will live in love for all eternity. There is no **'til death do us part**. Our souls are timeless.

Now, there are lessons to be learned. If it would work, I'm sure that God would let us learn these lessons without any pain and suffering, but the real lessons in life are not taught to us by people or experiences that come too easily. If you are too comfortable in life, you are standing still. The times in your life that you remember as terribly hard or painful are the true gifts because they are the catalysts for growth.

We cross paths with many people during our visit to Earth and experience something with each and every one we meet. None of them are accidents or mistakes or coincidences. Some people stay for only a few seconds and some for many years. Although you might believe that you could have changed things had you done something just slightly differently, you probably couldn't have. Your relationship with God is between you and Him. The path was decided upon before it began. There is a reason for all that you experience.

Once I realized this, life became much easier to understand and experience. If you turn your life over to God and promise Him that you will accept whatever comes your way, no matter what that may be, you will find a peace that will fill you to overflowing with love and joy.

I think back on what has happened to me, on things that I have considered to be punishments or tragedies and now see that they were actually lessons.

My mother was a lesson. At her funeral, I gave the eulogy and offended many of her friends and most of my family. I said that she was a "pain in the ass" and that she hadn't been the mother that I would have asked for had I been able to choose — although I now believe that I more than likely actually did chose her. I also spoke of the good memories I had. Everyone else said all the usual kind things you say at funerals, but I had to speak my truth. I had come to peace with my mother long before that day and I knew that she would understand and accept what I was saying about her because I now understood why she had treated me as she had. She was a gift in disguise and she had chosen to be my mother to teach me something very important. I said that I loved her very much and wanted to thank her for sacrificing her life to be one of my greatest teachers. You see, she taught me about jealousy and the pain it can cause and all the things she didn't give me are exactly what has made me a more loving and compassionate person. For that I am truly grateful.

Then there was my father, who taught me the lesson of secrecy. I spent a long time on this lesson and somewhere in my 50's I think I might have finally taken the exam for the last time. God bless him. I know he did what he felt he had to do to keep the peace. He had six kids and a wife who was capable of making life miserable if things didn't go her way. I can't say that I wouldn't have done things exactly the same way he had under the same circumstances. His examples of secrecy in action were what shaped the woman I became. As awful as it was while it was happening, I can now look back an see the lesson. I am raising Sean and Brittany in a honest environment. No one ever has to feel unloved in our house. I no longer say what I think they want to hear, but what I think will help them become better human beings. Sometimes the truth is hard to hear, but there is no place in my life for secrecy. Thanks Dad for the gift of honesty.

Except for Steve, I would have to say that Kym was my greatest lesson. She taught me the lesson of knowing when to walk away. I love this only child of mine with all my heart and soul and a day never goes by that I don't pray for her and wonder if she is okay. I can't even begin to imagine what lesson she is learning from her life. She was abandoned by her biological father at birth, was raised to be completely dependent upon her over indulgent mother, couldn't accept sharing her mother with her new step-father and became a very emotionally upset teenager, who turned to substance abuse and abusive men to try and fill her void. She is alone without her parents, her children, her grandparents or any of the other relatives that come with a family. The last time I saw her she was in an abusive relationship from which she couldn't escape because she didn't know how to take care of herself and didn't have anyone else to turn to for help. She has burnt all her bridges and my heart cries for her every night. I have learned that I should have let her go a long time ago so that she could move on down her path. I can't live her life for her. It is between her and God.

Yet teaching me to let go was not the only gift she has given me. What greater sacrifice could anyone make than to give up their own children to help someone else. Perhaps it appeared that she did it to make life easier for herself, but I believe that she decided to do this for me long before she came down to Earth. There isn't anything that she has done that could be terrible enough for her to deserve the pain she must feel on a daily basis. She has lost her mother and her children. When I feel abandoned and alone, I only need to think of her losses and mine seem pale in comparison. Thank you God for the gift of Kym.

I can't very well thank God for Kym and not thank Him for the man who made it possible for me to have her. All the other negative things about him are somehow cancelled out by the many blessings that were given to me because he stopped by my life to impregnate me with our child. Without him, there would be no Kym, which means there would be no Sean or Brittany. Thank you, Bill, for all of my children.

My high school sweetheart was a lesson I won't soon forget. Although he broke my heart, he taught me about passion and helped me discover my sexuality. I was a mere child when I met him and because I loved him first and was young and inexperienced, I loved him without reservation. I was so lucky to be able to share this precious moment with someone who was tender and gentle at such a young age. Every man I was ever with after him benefited from the lessons we learned together. Like many other women, I will always have a special corner in my heart for this boy who changed me into a woman.

In my search to understand the lesson I learned from Dr. Keller, I learned an important lesson about virtue from His Holiness The Dalai Lama. The dictionary defines virtue as: conformity to moral law; a commendable quality. I believe you cannot be virtuous unless you understand what it means to be compassionate. The Dalai Lama speaks of cultivating compassion for people irrespective of whether or not we have direct relationships with them. He says that, those who attain great learning but lack a good heart are in danger of being incapable of fulfillment. Having knowledge without compassion leads to an attitude towards others which is likely to be a mixture of envy of those in positions above you, aggressive competitiveness toward your peers and scorn for those less fortunate. This leads to a propensity toward greed, presumption, excess, and, very quickly, to loss of happiness. Knowledge is important, but much more so is the use toward which it is put. This depends on the heart and mind of the one who uses it. He adds that compassion is not a luxury. It is fundamental to inner peace. With it comes forgiveness and tolerance. It gives meaning to our daily lives. There is nothing amazing about being educated or wealthy. It is only when you also have developed what he calls a "warm heart" that these attributes become worthwhile. For these lessons I thank the Dalai Lama.

It took me a long time to find compassion in my heart for Dr. Keller. It took me even longer to put the pain of my loss and anger aside and replace it with understanding. I have no idea what has made him the doctor that he is. I have learned to try and understand him as he is and not as I wish he would have been. The only way for me to find peace with the tragedy that he has caused our family is to stop judging him and see him as a fellow human being who I might actually have admired or respected under a different set of circumstances. I don't have to embrace him, but, in order to find my own inner peace, I have forgiven him. I can only hope that someday he will understand what he has done and it will help him to develop a "warm heart" and "ethical wholesomeness" in the profession he has chosen.

So, here's something I thought I'd never say. Thank you Dr. Keller for teaching me the lessons of virtue, compassion and forgiveness. The struggle to forgive you has taught me so much about myself.

Then, of course, there is Jim. I'm sure he doesn't know it, but he was probably the one who was most responsible for my new outlook on life. The guilt that came from our affair was undoubtedly what forced me to finally work so hard to figure out why I had such a terrible void in my life. It's been many years since the last time I talked to him and I won't say that I don't think about him and wonder how he is doing, but I never call. That is all part of my past now. I could not be "just a friend" to a man I had been intimate with no matter how I tried to convince myself I could. When the opportunity arose and I was tempted to cross that invisible line I had drawn in the sand, it was too easy to step over it. He and all other married men are off limits. Besides, I no longer need a secret relationship to fill my emptiness. That void no longer exists. It has been filled by personal integrity and the peace that it brings.

I am still learning lessons because of him though. Awhile back, an old acquaintance of mine called to tell me that she had found out her husband had been seeing someone else behind her back for the past few years. She had been clueless and she was devastated by her discovery. We spent hours talking on the phone and in person and via e-mail. As I listened to her explain the pain her husband's affair caused her, I was forced to admit that I might, very well, have inflicted that same pain on someone else. I told her about my affair and she asked me questions about whether or not we talked about his wife and how involved I was in his day-to-day decisions. She showed me through her pain how much I was taking away from his relationship with his wife by letting him turn to me instead of her when he needed to talk about things that were bothering him or when he needed help making major decisions in his life.

Listening to my friend's anger, pain, self-doubt and disappointment taught me so much about commitment. It is a very damaging thing to turn to someone other than your spouse to find comfort when your life is in turmoil. It is the coward's way out. It is easy to tell someone you are sexually involved with about a problem in your life. They may or may not have the answer, but what you remember the most is how wonderful it felt to be intimate with that person. They seem so perfect. Well, of course, they do. They don't have to go home with you and live in the real world. They don't have to live up to their solutions because they won't be involved in them. The real test would be to have the courage to go to your spouse and talk things out. When you turn to someone else, you cheat your partner of the opportunity to share that moment with you. He or she isn't on equal ground with your lover because they don't even know that there is a problem, let alone that they have been denied the opportunity to help you work through it. What a terrible thing to do to someone you vowed to be committed to for the rest of your life.

I used to try and tell myself that I helped their marriage because I helped him get through the tough times. But now, because of my friend's situation, I was forced once again to see that it wasn't just about me and how my life was affected by what I had done. I was shown the pain from the wife's vantage point. It helped me see things with greater clarity and finally take off the blinders I had been wearing for so long. By sharing her pain, I could no longer pretend that what I had done wasn't hurting anyone else. For the first time, I saw what we had done to our respective spouses. So, not only was "he" a lesson, but so was my friend. Hard, painful, shameful, valuable lessons.

There were many "easy" lessons for which I am grateful, like my good friends and loving family. They were not so much lessons as gifts. They kept me on my path and reminded me that I was loved and needed. What a miserable place this school of life would be if we didn't have our gifts of easy lessons.

There was one person who came into my life for both the easy and hard parts. No one will ever know how truly blessed I was to share so much of my life with him. Some people say that there is no such thing as a soul mate. That may be so, but Steve was as close as you could come to being one. I am certain that I have known Steve since the beginning of time and I know that we will be together forever. Maybe not as the same two people that we were here on Earth, but surely as whatever we become when we move on to the next part of our lives. I have never and will never love anyone as much as I love him. The joy he brought me was immeasurable. I only wish I had known then what I know now, but then what would the purpose have been.

What lessons did he teach me? Well, first, he taught me about unconditional love. He taught me to love someone completely without reservations. No doubts, no what-ifs, no past mistakes, no future concerns, no holding back just in case the other person doesn't love you back. No "I'll love you when I'm certain that you won't abandon me." He loved me with all my faults. He loved me enough that he was able to allow me to make the wrong decisions in order to learn from my mistakes. He loved me so much that he was willing to accept whatever pain I might cause him while I was fumbling with my struggle to become whole. He taught me that being cautious might just be the biggest risk you ever take.

He taught me that I can be whole all by myself. I don't need anyone to complete me. It was fun sharing my life with him and it made life much more enjoyable having him as a partner. Certainly, he was the icing, but I was the cake. He made my life sweeter, but it could have been delicious all alone too. Everything I always needed was already inside me if only I'd taken the time to look. I never knew that, but now I do.

But the most important lesson he taught me was the answer to John's question about why God allows us to suffer. Through his dying and the suffering that followed, Steve motivated me to remember from where I came and to where I will someday return. Without the pain and the guilt and the depression that I experienced after his death, I would have never been motivated to find out the reason for the void I have been living with all my life. He showed me that God allows us to suffer so that we will move on to the next level. It is possible to be motivated by something wonderful, but nothing moves you forward quite like the devastation of losing someone you love. When you hit the bottom and you look up to Heaven and say, "I can't do this, Lord. Please help me. Answer my prayer," you ask Him to come into your life. That is what He has been waiting for all this time. By this simple request, we open the flood gates and allow His love to fill us.

Some of God's greatest gifts are, indeed, unanswered prayers. I hear so many people say, "I know there is no God because I prayed to him about this or that and I never get what I asked for." Well, my answer to that is that you probably were asking for the wrong thing because you didn't see the larger picture. What is happening isn't just happening to you. It is happening to the entire universe and you are just one small piece of the puzzle. Your part might not make sense until the puzzle is complete.

Now when I pray, I try to ask God to guide me or I ask for patience or understanding or strength or assistance in trying to live a more spiritual life. I trust Him because I know that He knows what I need, be it joyful or painful, and then I tell Him how grateful I am that He has blessed me with the experience. I try never to attach an expectation to my prayer.

Steve was my most wonderful lesson and my most painful lesson all wrapped up into one. Our time together was very special and I can only hope that just one person reads this book and "gets it" when they see that I am living proof that life's most rewarding gifts sometimes come out of the depths of despair.

My void was filled by the love of God Himself. The love that was always there, but which had been momentarily forgotten. The love that I had sometimes been denied by my biological father has been given to me at long last by my Heavenly Father. This relationship with God is expressed beautifully in the words of C. Austin Miles in his hymn "In The Garden,"

And He walks with me,
And He talks with me,
And He tells me I am His own;
And the joy we share as we tarry there
None other has ever known.

ℰ Epilogue ℰ

I wrote this book off and on from 1998 through 2001 and, for those three years it was the therapy that I needed to become whole again. Then I set it aside on a shelf and really didn't give it much thought again until just recently. I got it out, dusted it off and read it again and was amazed that I might have actually put together something worthy of sharing with others.

It has now been eight years since Steve's death and much has happened in the last few years that aren't included in my book. I did pursue legal action against Steve's doctor. It took two years of constant struggle and when we were just about ready to go to trial, the other side offered to settle out of court. My counsel felt we had a very strong case and were willing to go ahead with the trial, but I told them to take the settlement. It was minimal compared to the love that was taken away when we lost Steve. However, it was never really about the money anyway. I wanted Dr. Keller to understand the impact he had on our lives and hoped that the knowledge he gained from reviewing Steve's medical history might help make him a more conscientious doctor and, more importantly, a better man. I'll never know what affect it had on him, but I put it out there and the rest was up to him. When it was all over, I finally put my grief to rest and that was vitally important to my moving forward with my life.

After years of separation, Kym came back into our lives again. She divorced Joe and came and lived with us for a short while which gave us all some closure. The kids are teenagers now and are old enough to understand what happened from both perspectives and seem to have a pretty good handle on things. For the first time in our lives, she and I were able to be completely honest and face the pain we had knowingly or unknowingly caused each other during our lives together as mother and daughter. It has made a great deal of difference in our relationship to be able to say "I love you, but that doesn't always mean I have to agree with you." She is married to a nice man now and I enjoy watching her start this new part of her life.

Oprah's still on television. Besides her show, she's got a magazine and a website and now she is over in Africa helping build schools and improve the lives of the children there. She is my mentor and the most amazing woman I have ever known. She changed my life. Steve's death was my tragedy, the affair was my mistake, this book was my instrument for healing and, hopefully, the vehicle by which I fulfill my reason for being here; but, if I hadn't been lying on that couch in my pajamas stuffing Ho Hos down my throat that day watching Oprah's show, I might never have gotten the message. Thanks again, Oprah, for doing what you do everyday. You make a difference.

Speaking of "getting it," I'm sure you already know this, but Dr. Phil did get his own show and he's doing a weight loss challenge right now and I sure could use it. Iyanla Vanzant is a life coach on a new show called "Starting Over" that helps woman dig deep inside themselves and find the courage to face their problems head on and learn life's lessons. I see Wayne Dyer on PBS every so often speaking about "The Power of Intention." My teachers are still teaching.

Thank you for taking the time to read my book. I hope you enjoyed reading it as much as I enjoyed writing it. I can only pray that it will help you find the peace that reconnecting with God has brought me.

If nothing else, I hope I have encouraged you to go on living when it seems as though you can't. There is life after death and not just for those who have passed on. Whatever your loss, no matter the cause — death, divorce, failing health, career setbacks, addiction or anything, don't give up. Rise to the challenge and learn from your loss.

CPSIA information can be obtained
at www.ICGtesting.com
Printed in the USA
LVHW081322070921
697210LV00026B/627